# HOW TO
## FIND WORK...
## and Keep Finding Work
## for the Rest of Your Life

## BY "DR. CHAZ"
## Charles Michael Austin, Ed.D.

Printed by CreateSpace

Library of Congress Cataloging-in-Publication Data

ISBN: 1468172182
ISBN-13: 9781468172188`

*For Monica*

*Having been your husband*
*for the past few years*
*has taught me*
*that Lou Gehrig was the **second** luckiest man*
*on the face of the earth.*

# TABLE OF CONTENTS

# INTRODUCTION

*The mediocre teacher tells. The good teacher explains.*
*The superior teacher demonstrates. The great teacher inspires.*
*–William Arthur Ward*

There is a sign in my office that says, "Welcome to the Tough Love Dispensary."

Well, reader, welcome to my office—in book form. *How to Find Work... And Keep Finding Work for the Rest of Your Life* is straight talk on how to deal with the working world the way it really is, not how we'd like it to be. As a career mentor and educator who is dedicated to preparing my clients to be successful, to supporting and empowering them to make their dreams come true, I can do no less. There are things in this book that you may not *want* to hear, but I believe you *need* to hear (or, more accurately, *read*). As it says in *my* Bible, "The truth shall set you free, but first it's going to piss you off."

Whatever your vocational goals, whatever stage you're in in your career—from just beginning to close-to-retiring-but-you-can't-afford-to-stop-making-money—this book will help you get from here to there, turning your dreams and fantasies into actions and results. I'm known among my colleagues as "the human alarm clock" because I wake people up to what's possible in themselves and in the world. I hold three degrees: a BA in Sociology, an MA in Broadcast Communication Arts (Radio and Television), and an EdD in Organizational Leadership, and I've worked with literally hundreds of clients and students, from teenagers to adults in their sixties, at fourteen—and counting—different colleges and universities. I know that, with the exception of retirees who "always wanted to take a film course" at their local community college, all students go to school for primarily one reason: to increase their earning power.

Everything I teach, and everything in this book, is designed to impart practical, relevant knowledge[1*] and practices that you can use forever to help you make more money doing satisfying, fulfilling work that you love (or at least enjoy).

The foundation of all the training and coaching I do is called Experiential Learning. It's best expressed in a quote from Aristotle: "We are what we repeatedly do. Excellence, then, is not an act, but a habit." I believe we learn best by *doing*—over and over and over again. Experiential Learning focuses on discovering by doing, instead of just hearing or reading about the experiences of others. In school, most of use used rote learning (also called cognitive or didactic learning), the goal of which is to have the teacher transmit information to the student. "Open head, pour in information, close head," as my friend Dr. Elizabeth Trebow describes it.

Experiential Learning, on the other hand, is about meaningful, immersive, and *long-lasting* learning. It's knowledge that's relevant, pervasive, and *applied*. It develops muscle memory, so it sticks with you.

---

1      * I deliberately use the word "knowledge" rather than "information." We have a lot of *information* about the activities of celebrities but, while gossip is fun, this *information* doesn't improve our lives. *Knowledge*, on the other hand, is something we can use to better ourselves. As Yale librarian Rutherford D. Rogers put it, "We're drowning in information and starving for knowledge."

# PART ONE:

# FOR THE JOBSEEKER

*No other technique for the conduct of life attaches the individual so firmly to reality as laying emphasis on work, for his work at least gives him a secure place in a portion of reality, in the human community.*
*—Sigmund Freud*

## CHAPTER ONE

# THE WORLD OF WORK, THEN

*The world is not to be put in order; the world is order,*
*incarnate. It is for us to harmonize with this order.*
*—Henry Miller*

*You practice and you get better. It's very simple.*
*—Philip Glass*

A long time ago in a galaxy far, far away…oh wait, that's the opening to *Star Wars*. Way back in the twentieth century, an education consisted of course after course after course, eventually leading to a diploma or degree. Sadly, not much has changed. Many people still wonder why they worked so hard and for so long, spent so much time and money, and what they received in return for all that, besides debt.

In the twentieth century, getting an interview was all about submitting a good resume and a strong cover letter and then waiting to hear back. We are still stuck in this paradigm. It worked back then, but it no longer applies.

## AND NOW

The working world has changed dramatically in the past few years. Why have things changed? A number of factors have contributed to this shift, and short-term thinking is a major one.

Since shareholders began demanding that stock prices continually climb higher than they had the previous quarter, emphasis has changed from long-term gain to *short-term* profitability and *short-term* strategies. If you run a company, you have to look for ways to increase profits at all times, and the two ways to do that are to increase revenue and cut expenses.

Let's create a fictitious company. We'll call it ZYX. If you're the CEO, and ZYX is part of a mature industry in which there's little chance of increasing market share every year, let alone every quarter, your option is to cut expenses. What's the most expensive item in any company? Personnel; that's where the cutting starts.

Now let's say you're a ZYX employee. You may suddenly be perceived to be expendable. "But yesterday they said I was a valuable asset," you protest.

Wake up. Money considerations outweigh almost everything else. The CEO is not a bad person; you'd probably behave exactly the same way in his or her position. A CEO needs to look at whether they can find someone who costs less to do your job. Nothing personal. The company "cares" about you to the extent that you are an a$$et to them; when you begin to be perceived as a liability, you're on your way out the door.

Health insurance can add 30 percent to the cost of an employee's salary. Let's take that one step further. The CEO thinks he or she might as well just hire people on a contract or project basis. Why should the company keep paying employees a salary when they're not busy? Why not just hire them for as long as they're needed? The production side of the entertainment industry has been using temp workers for most of their staffing needs since the studio system was dismantled beginning in the late 1940s.

People are hired on an "as needed" basis, and as soon as the project is over, they're gone.

The rest of the labor market, too, is going in this direction. It's no wonder there's an increasing use of:

- Outsourcing. The outsourcing industry has grown about 10 percent every year since 2005 and now has a market value of about $600 billion.
- Offshoring. An estimated one million jobs now held by Americans will be offshored by 2014. That's on top of an estimated three million manufacturing jobs that have been lost since 1998 and 500,000 service and IT jobs that have moved overseas in recent years.
- Temps, contract workers, and consultants. Close to ten million are hired in the United States every year, and only about 80 percent of them work full time.

It's no surprise that the power of unions has been declining. In 2010 the U.S. Bureau of Labor Statistics reported that 11.9 percent of workers were members of a union, down from 12.3 percent a year earlier. In 1983 (the first year for which comparable data are available), the union membership rate was 20.1 percent.

If you're entering or re-entering the workforce—after losing a job, changing careers, or finishing school—these are some of the circumstances you can look forward to. Their inevitable results: downsizing, layoffs, and early retirement.[2]* Every time I read about a merger, I know the next bit of news will be that the new company is cutting its workforce.

More and more workers are on their own now, and it's important that you understand and prepare yourself.

---

2        * Don't you love all the euphemisms for "we don't want you here anymore"? Human beings have a hard time with confrontation and want neither to receive—nor to give—bad news. It's easier for the bad news *givers* if they try to soften the blow with language other than "You're fired." We can't all be Donald Trump.

## THE IMPACT OF TECHNOLOGY ON THE WORKPLACE

Back in the olden days, say twenty to thirty years ago, there were a couple of job titles called "assistant" and "secretary." These people would do the grunt work for managers and executives—the typing, filing, et cetera. Today, in the age of laptops and iPads and smartphones, we're all doing that work for ourselves. And because of these hi-tech handcuffs, we're available to work more hours. Employers are only too happy to take advantage of this fact—and of you.

We all are doing the work of at least two people, and your boss is, too. If you work for a company that has had layoffs and you were lucky enough to keep your job, you've now taken on the work of those who were let go. You may be doing the work of *three or four* people, being paid for just one, and grateful to have a job at all!

Let's set the scene, as we say in Hollywood. Let's say an employer has a job opening and posts it. And in response come five hundred to a thousand resumes. That figure is not an exaggeration; a colleague of mine who is an executive with The Walt Disney Company was amazed to receive five hundred resumes for an assistant position. Human Resources told him, "That's nothing. The record for a job opening at Disney is fourteen thousand resumes!"

I was involved in digital media for about ten years, starting in the early 1990s—even before there was an Internet. We early adopters felt that digital media would change everything, and so it has. Many things that people counted on as the foundations of their lives in the mid twentieth century are becoming unrecognizable or have simply disappeared: commercial radio, newspapers, magazines, phone books, the Big Three auto makers, the dominance of the three television broadcast networks.

Technology was supposed to make us more productive, and it has. It was also supposed to free us up to have more leisure time. Is that true for you? Or are you working more and getting paid less for your time? Technology promised freedom but delivered something akin to slavery. From ZYX's perspective, technology means the company can get more out of its workers for less money; it's very efficient and cost-effective to have workers chained to their electronic leashes and available for work 24/7.

## TODAY, WE ARE ALL FREELANCERS

Corporate loyalty is becoming less and less common. You— all of us— are freelancers now and for the foreseeable future. According to the American Heritage Dictionary, a freelancer is "a person who sells services to employers without a long-term commitment to any of them." The lack of availability of full-time jobs with benefits makes it imperative that you start thinking of yourself as a freelancer. You will need to learn how to sell yourself and the services, expertise, and experience you offer.

Employers can't afford to care about your long-term needs. You've no doubt heard the expression "It's business; it's not personal." Well, believe it; it's true. No matter how much your boss may like you, no matter how many awards, raises, and great performance reviews you've received, no matter how long you've worked there, *you are expendable at a moment's notice.* Don't get comfortable. Think of yourself as rented furniture—you'll be returned to where you came from when you're no longer of use. And it can happen at any time, often due to factors beyond your control and despite the great job you've been doing.

I'm not assuming that the advice I'm giving you will go down easy. I realize a lot of what I'm telling you runs counter to conventional wisdom. You may be at what I call a Resistance Point, which is a moment when I tell you something, and you say, "Whoa, wait a minute! That can't be right. I can't—or won't— do that."

But I've done this work for many years and with great success. You may not believe in or want to do the things I suggest, but I promise that they work.

I know you don't *want* to freelance. For most people, the thought of having to constantly sell themselves to strangers for the rest of their lives is abhorrent. Many people argue that their

7

parents worked for one company their entire lives and then retired with a pension, and they want to know why they don't get to do the same thing. The bad news is that pensions are rapidly becoming a relic of another era, and it's gotten tougher to save enough money for retirement.

As the expression goes, "You can't know where you're going until you know where you're at." So now that you have some sense of the employment landscape, let's look at how you can successfully navigate it.

# CHAPTER TWO

# IDENTIFYING YOUR PASSION

*Man's desires are limited by his perceptions;*
*none can desire what he has not perceived.*
*–William Blake*

*Nothing is really work unless you would rather*
*be doing something else.*
*–James M. Barrie*

*Follow your joy.*
*–Joseph Campbell*

*Just go out there and have fun...*
*If you're having fun, the money will come.*
*–Willie Mays*

Though it may seem odd, let's start at the end. What do *you* want to do? What's your passion—that thing you love to do for hours on end that you can get lost in, that puts you in "the zone," that makes you forget to eat or has you lose track of what time it is. As Confucius said, "I am a person who forgets his food when engaged in vigorous pursuit of something." Your passion is the wellspring of everything we'll do together and how you'll shape your career.

You may have tried to determine your passion before, only to end up frustrated ("I just can't figure out what I want to do!"). If you don't know exactly what your passion is, *don't worry about it.* Spending a lot of time trying to figure out exactly what it is you want to do, or are *meant* to do, or are *supposed* to do can be a waste of time. I know I differ from a lot of career coaches and counselors in this regard, like Dick Bolles, author of *What Color Is Your Parachute,* and fans of the Myers-Briggs Personality Test and others like it. But the truth is the "new normal" is that you'll have multiple careers; it's predicted that Millennials will have five or six of them! Since you will most likely have more than one career, the best way to find them is through the experience of working at things you enjoy or in which you think you may be interested. You will find your passion or passions eventually. Meanwhile, get to work and do something that interests you.

On the flip side, there are those of us who are lucky and *know* what they want to do. Next comes the question of what degrees, skills, and experience the career requires. Of course, over time the goals of these careers may change, and when they do, so will the requirements.

I attended the High School of Music and Art in New York. It later merged with the High School of Performing Arts (from the movie *Fame*) and is now known as the Fiorello H. LaGuardia High School of Music & Art and Performing Arts. Students there take a full academic course load plus a major in music or art— my major was voice. When I graduated, my father said, "Okay, enough nonsense. It's time to get serious. You need to become a businessman." So I started college at the Baruch School of Business of The City College of New York, which is now known simply as Baruch College. By the end of my first semester, I had flunked both economics and accounting and found myself on academic probation.

It was time for a serious reappraisal of my direction in higher education. I told my dad, "We tried it your way. It didn't work. I have no interest in the financial side of business, so I'm switching majors." I became a sociology major and my GPA vastly improved during my last three years of college. So though they do want you to be happy, it's not what your parents want you to do that really matters.

Nor does it matter what your peers are doing. Every few years, there's a new, hot, flavor-of-the-month industry. Recently it's been law; finance (leading millions of people to get their MBAs); health care; green energy; and so on. Certainly all these careers are worth looking at, but just because that's where your peers are going and where the money is at the time doesn't mean it's the right field for you.

## WHERE TO LOOK TO FIND YOUR PASSION

What are you good at in school, at work, at play?
What are your talents and interests?
What have you always wanted to try or learn more about?

What Marsha Sinetar says is true: "Do what you love and the money will follow." So if you don't know what it is you love, the place to start is with what you think you'd *like* and eventually you'll fall in love. It's kind of like dating, which we'll touch on later.

Don't base your career direction solely on what the Wall Street Journal or any other publication says is paying well. Most people would like to have a lot of money and all the things it can buy. But don't have greed be your primary motivator; it's not going to be enough to carry you to success.

Sure, I will admit to using greed as a way to motivate my clients. But instead of *starting* with the money, I start with identifying the passion; the money becomes the inevitable bonus. Greed gets their attention. Next comes empowering them to become what they dream of being.

## MONETIZEABLE PASSION

Whether your passion is monetizeable is a hugely important distinction. Just because you love it doesn't mean you can make a living at it. The poet Wallace Stevens sold insurance, as did the composer Charles Ives. I had a friend who worked for Nielsen Ratings for over thirty years. Was it her passion? No, she said. It was her *job*. Her passion was horses, and the money she made at her job funded the passion.

I'm not saying you have to sell insurance. But if, for example, you're a painter and your oil paintings don't cover your bills, work at something related that you can enjoy—or at least tolerate—like working for a graphic design firm. You can use some of your artistic skills at your job, and paint at night and on weekends.

Some people, like Bobby Colomby, have to make a choice. He once told me there were two things he loved to do: playing basketball and playing the drums. Since he was only six feet tall, he knew he'd never get into the NBA, so he became a drummer instead. He later founded Blood, Sweat and Tears, one of the seminal groups of the jazz rock genre, and was considered one of the top drummers of his era.

When you find your passion, you'll need to determine if it's monetizeable. In other words, can you make money from it? Will someone pay for your skills? Are the industries or companies you want to work for hiring now?

## STORIES OF PASSION AND PLANNING

You'll know you've found your passion when you'll do whatever it takes to get you where you want to go. It's the difference between involvement and commitment. Take this plate of ham and eggs for example:

The chicken is *involved*. The pig is *committed*.

Mike was a student I worked with at Pepperdine University. He came into my office one day with what he thought might be a problem. He was being considered for a management training program with a well-known multinational corporation. The problem was that he was a Canadian citizen, the company was American, and he thought the fact that he couldn't legally work in the United States might disqualify him. His girlfriend was American and they were planning to get married in a few months, which would grant him American citizenship, but he thought the company might not want to wait.

I asked him why, if he and his girlfriend were going to get married, did they need to wait, and I suggested they marry right away. Mike found this idea outrageous, but I challenged him about how much he wanted the job.

He thought it over, came back into my office the next morning, stretched out his hand and said, "Congratulate me. I got engaged last night!"

Mike was accepted into the management training program.

What are the experiences of others who found their passion? What did they do after they found it? And what about those who don't pursue their passion?

*Franklin G. Strauss, M.D.*

I spent a lot of time planning my career. In my teenage years, I was quite certain about choosing medicine, which meant I had to get my act together to attend an excellent college and plan my college curriculum so that I could be a potential medical student. During medical school, I had to carefully consider internship options. After that, I had to choose my residency, decide on a specialty, and plan how to position myself to be selected by a good nephrology fellowship program. After all this and two years in the military were completed, I had to select between various types of positions in academia, private practice, hospital practice, et cetera. A passion may require lots of planning to finally arrive at a favorable position.

As to how to do the planning, at each stage one can benefit from consulting "role models," communicating with peers at the same stage, and questioning people several years ahead for suggestions and feedback. Any benefits? Couldn't have done it without all that effort in planning. No other possible answer.

*Sam Glick, Promotion/Marketing Executive, Entrepreneur and former Talent Agent*

Planning my career was something I began thinking about as an adolescent. Of course, the final form it takes today was not what I envisioned then. I never measured my plans in hours, days, weeks, years. It's an evolutionary process, some stages with more verve than others. I remember well the time spent planning to find a job within the career. My theory on that was if I wanted a full-time job, then I'd better spend full time looking for it.

In high school, planning my career meant finding a college that would facilitate a pathway into communications. During college, it meant exposing myself to experiences that were all communications related—summer jobs, people with similar interests, et cetera. But no matter how much I planned, the variables of life drastically altered my course: opportunity, failure, marriage, children. It's not so much the tangibles that went into how I planned my career but more the intangibles like determination, confidence, and knowledge about my industry and the people in it.

I think the best thing is to develop a loose game plan for yourself. Allow it the flexibility to travel in different directions. Expect it to have many forks in the road, so no matter which path you take, you won't be disappointed.

*Susan Love, M.D.*

Although my first reaction is that I do no planning, that is not entirely true. Every few years or so I write out a list of my long term goals, and then I figure out what steps are most likely to get me there. I remember an early list, from after I had just gone into practice, included becoming nationally well known. This among other things led me to specialize in breast cancer—which was not popular at the time, but an underserved niche—and to write my first book. My goal of becoming more fit has led me to running marathons—two done and another planned. These goals are not fixed, but they give me a general path and help me distribute my time. For example, early on when I wanted to be known by a broader audience, I accepted a lot of speaking engagements. My current goal is to firm up my academic credentials and make known my developments in ductal lavage. To accomplish these goals, I have to write more academic papers and do fewer lay activities for a while.

The key in my mind is to have general goals that are important to you, but to keep the steps flexible enough to get you there. For example, while working on my "eradicating breast cancer" goal by developing ductal lavage with university grants—a slow-going process—an opportunity arose to start a medical device company. I shifted my plan and was on the move much faster. It was beneficial not to have a goal as specific as "eradicate breast cancer by doing research at UCLA funded by the Department of Defense." The main purpose of goals is to help you at the crossroads. You should always be able to see other ways to get there.

*Larry Rubin, Lawrence Rubin, Ph.D. & Associates*

My overriding goal has always been to make as much money as possible, but only within the context of a job I enjoy, that includes intellectual substance, opportunities for personal validation, and good working conditions. In pursuit of this, I have generally been satisfied staying where I am until I become dissatisfied, rather than planning a career several steps ahead.

*Karen Bradbury*

Even at a young age I knew that I wanted to make money. My mother tells a story about my coming home from school and telling her I was going to drop out to work at 7-Eleven because they were paying $2.05 an hour. At nine years old, that was a lot of money.

When I was in junior high and high school, I wanted to be either a circus clown or run my own store or business. After learning that circus clowns made no money and lived on trains, I chose the business path.

When choosing a college, my focus was on attending a school that would not only provide a useful education, but that suited my needs as an individual. In hindsight, selecting a small school was an important part of my career planning.

Many people were concerned about my interest in running a retail store because of the long hours, personal attachment and the risk of failure. Their input helped focus my studies on marketing and advertising instead of merchandising. In the end, this path provided a broader range of knowledge which has been extremely valuable.

After college, I joined Macy's to get some retail experience. For several years, I worked my way up the ladder gaining valuable experience, studying competition both large and small as well as understanding that retail was truly a great deal of work, one reason few independent retailers have survived.

This is where my emphasis on marketing and advertising paid off. Owning a business might not have been an ideal fit, but running a business was a very appealing goal so I looked for a position that would help me get there. I found a great sales position and eighteen years later I'm still with the same company. My role is now brand president and it comes with a great deal of autonomy. While there are aspects of the business that have to be done to a "standard," I, with my team, make most all of the important decisions.

Identifying skills and passions as well as developmental and performance needs at a young age were all key. Using them to select a career path certainly paid off. I believe the secret, while not easy, is finding something you enjoy and then building a career around it. I'm a people person and that's why retail and sales caught my interest. It is also important to find a school and employer that fit your needs and personality. Studying who you are is important in defining who you will be.

*Monica Blauner*

I'm one of those people who always knew what they wanted to do. When I was twelve my friends told me that I was a good listener. My family was "therapy friendly." My mother had gone to therapy, and my uncle had trained to be a psychoanalyst. As a teenager I went to therapy myself, and I just knew that was what I wanted to do. My first semester in college, I took introduction courses in psychology and sociology and decided to major in psychology. The next question was whether to get a master's degree in social work or a PhD in psychology. I spoke to a psychology professor, and he suggested I consider getting an MD. I thought about that for about twenty-four hours before I said to myself, "Biochemistry?!" The answer clearly was no.

I decided on a social work degree because I liked the perspective of looking at the whole person. I had good grades and test scores in college, so I applied to the top clinical social work schools in the country. Due to my inexperience, I got into only my last choice school. To remedy that, I got a job as an attendant in a state hospital that was affiliated with Tufts University. It was the best experience of my professional career. After that, I got into my top two choices of graduate schools. Going to a top school with a national reputation stood me in good stead throughout my career.

When I began looking for jobs, more than one potential employer said they called me for an interview because of the school I attended. In one interview, the interviewer said the position involved a lot of writing, when she stopped and said, "You went to Smith so I know you can write." Networking with fellow alumnae was also very helpful, and I made good friends and colleagues through them.

My first job after getting my degree was in a drug and alcohol rehab. I didn't have a particular interest in that area, but the experience was invaluable for the rest of my career. It opened doors for me. While I was in training to become a psychoanalyst, a clinic was looking for an analyst to teach a course about addictions, and my experience at the rehab made me qualified. In the late eighties, a hospital was hiring an AIDS social worker. I knew I didn't want to do that, but I thought they might offer me something else once they had met me. And that's exactly what happened; I became an AIDS educator and discovered that I loved to teach and I was good at it. Since that time, every job I have gotten has been through someone that I knew or was introduced to by someone I knew. I have loved my career as a therapist and teacher and have gotten enormous gratification from being good at it.

*Jeff Parmet*

I spent no time planning my future. I didn't think much about the future because I was very focused on the present. I just did what I was expected to do: went to college, went to law school, found a job, got married, had children. I was taught that if I did these things, the rest would take care of itself, and it has! All I did was seize the opportunities in front of me, and with God's grace, I have had all the good things in life. I am thankful each and every day.

So though I did not plan my career, a lot of planning goes into making it successful. I'm talking about strategy, business plans. I'm not advocating the path I took; I envy those who have had a calling from an early age. My eldest son is a musician. He knew at age twelve that he would pursue music, and everything he has done in his life has been focused on that pursuit. He is passionate about his work, and though he makes very little money, he is doing what he loves. I, on the other hand, make good money, and I enjoy what I do because it is intellectually challenging and interesting to me. But I could just as easily do something else, whereas my son could not. I think both paths are valid. We just have to play the hand we're dealt, so long as we do something worthwhile.

*Judy Bernstein*

I spent forty-five years planning my future, always learning, adjusting, resetting new goals. Indefinite amount of time, as it's an on-going process. Still considering law school.

Planning my career—knew I needed a college education. Went thru the course catalogue and selected areas of interest wherein I had good grades. Then narrowed choices to those which presented the best career opportunities. Selected Speech & Language development and therapy. I was offered a job teaching speech to deaf kids. I taught deaf kids to talk. Loved that and went back for a Master's in Deaf Education. New programs were being developed correlating speech and reading, so I went back for more professional education. Learned about Dyslexia and Attention Deficit Disorder and the newest, cutting edge methodologies to teach reading. I was on the cusp of that boom, so I opened The Learning Connection, a private educational therapy center for Dyslexic and ADD kids.

Meanwhile, I dated a guy who was an economist and financial guru, and I learned about that world. Got bored with TLC and Speech Therapy, so I interviewed and was hired by Smith Barney, where they provided formal training in financials and investing. Still working in that field.

My interest in law school also was happenstance...I was involved in divorce litigation and found it fascinating. Represented myself and that sparked an interest in yet another potential career path.

What are the benefits of planning?

You cannot move forward without a plan. You MUST PLAN for your career and your life. Things happen which may change your direction, but you cannot flounder while waiting for the world to come to you.

*Leslie Andrews, RDH, MBA*

My career change from corporate to dental hygiene came as an epiphany. I had been "stuck" in middle management for over ten years, even after completing my MBA. At the age of forty, I opened myself up mentally and psychically for change, so that when dental hygiene became a possibility, I didn't question it.

I did my research and called every dentist and dental hygienist I knew and asked them about satisfaction, hours, benefits, salary, and career longevity. All the reviews were positive, but they warned of the potential for burn out. Since I tend to take situations and put creative spins on them, I felt I could prevent burnout for myself. I also felt that my unique, eclectic background in theater and business would make a difference.

I made the decision in February of 1989 and I started the two year program that September, graduating and getting licensed in 1991.

I began full-time clinical dental hygiene in a single-dentist office. The next epiphany came when I started attending continuing education courses and it struck me as something I could do well. After that, I enjoyed a ten-year career as a professional educator, which allowed me to lecture nationally, author journal articles, and write the first continuing education course introducing alternative medicine to the dental community. When I tired of the travel and work load, dental hygiene afforded me the opportunity to go back to clinical work for as little time or as few days as I liked.

My take-home message is that, if you allow yourself to be flexible and go after something you believe will bring out your best qualities, everything else seems to fall into place.

*Linda Rheinstein*

I "fell" into my career, beginning with junior college and working for my father's production company (named after me) as he was divorcing and leaving NBC after 20 plus years to marry his secretary from his DC office. I also took a weekend and night internship at Video Tape Enterprises, the largest mobile unit company at the time. I was learning about the Tech...from cameras to Technical Director to audio to "Chyron" (or Datavision in those days). And bottom line, I hated school and was enjoying "the Biz," so my Dad made me an offer to take my college money and allow me to invest and start a business with him which we called "Autographics," named by Dick Clark whom I was working with at the time on a project. From there we grew to be the largest graphics rental business in the world with offices in NY and London, working on basically every major sporting event in the world.

In the 90's I went into partnership at The Post Group to start the first Digital Graphics and Special Effects Division with the first Aurora (the first Digital Paint System before the Quantel Paint Box). TGP Digital Center did very well, and we also opened Electric Paint during that time, which was another partnership between me, TPG and a man named Tony Redhead. We were the first to do "Digital One Sheets"—movie posters on a Hi End Paint Box.

We sold Electric Paint. I then left TPG to go back to Autographics...we did a rename and new mission for the company, On Air On Line, to pursue just that: on air on line projects. The first was the NFL on Fox. The whole On Air On Line look and feel happened when Fox took the NFL away from CBS.

I have been blessed to do some awesome projects to date. EVERY stage of my career has been TOTALLY unplanned, and now, due to an illness my passion lies with my foundation [idoggiebag.org] and using all my years of TV and Biz knowledge to try and do some good whilst doing good myself. So that's my quick story. NOOOO plans, just mostly trying to see opportunities, trying to listen to those around me - and my gut.

*Tom Lenzo, Consultant, Pasadena, CA*

My career has spanned almost four decades. At various times during that career, I thought about it. At other times, I let it happen, and often got lucky.

In the beginning, my parents simply said, "Go to college. Don't work in a factory like us." I was the second in my extended immigrant family to go to college. I completed a BA with a major in English and a minor in education, because my family always had a high respect for education and teachers. Unable to find a teaching job when I graduated, I enlisted in the Air Force, more to avoid working in a factory than as a career move.

In the Air Force, I got lucky in that I was assigned to the staff of a management training center. Since the attitude there centered around education, I used tuition reimbursement to take lots of classes at the local universities.

After the Air Force, I worked in two public schools where I made three career-planning decisions: first, I went to grad school while continuing to work; second, I got involved in the local training professional group; and third, I took a job as a training manager at almost three times what I was earning at the school. I left public schools to work in corporate training and never looked back.

After being laid off four years later from the "real job," I decided to take a class on how to be a consultant. There I learned that no matter what you do, you work for yourself. I have always applied that philosophy to my career and personal decisions.

Over the years, I often made career decisions regarding which projects to go after based on the client and the contents. One such decision was to turn down a permanent job offer at a government agency. Perhaps I could have retired a couple of years ago had I taken the job, but I would have lost my soul to their work environment.

Over the years, I stayed in certain niches and played to my strengths; that has benefited me. I also have been active in several professional organizations as a source of knowledge and networking. If an organization stopped meeting my needs, I left. If I had unmet needs, I started a new organization. I continue to learn via seminars, webinars, meetings, and conferences, which definitely benefit my career.

Some career decisions I made were due to being in the right place at the right time. A stop at a Xerox store led to the first of many consulting projects on Xerox's leading edge technology. Bumping into a neighbor who told me about a PC user group at Caltech. I can't begin to explain the influence that chance meeting and my subsequent involvement in the user group had on my career.

Four decades and I'm still looking forward to the next project, the next client, the next learning experience. I didn't plan it, but I am satisfied.

# CHAPTER THREE

# THE EMPLOYER'S PERSPECTIVE

*The customer is the most important part of the production line.*
*—W. Edwards Deming*

Once we have determined your passion, or at least your direction, the first thing we look at is the employer's perspective. I help my clients package their education, skills, and experience, and the employer is who will exchange money for that package. The *employer* is your customer.

Keep in mind the golden rule: *Whoever has the gold makes the rules.* Yes, I know that other golden rule, but we're talking business here. Bosses are not your enemy; have some compassion for the person on the other side of the table. Your focus should be on the employer's needs and what you can do for them. Always remember: employers are primarily interested in what you've done that can make or save them money. And your goal is to find the people who have the money. Your strategy is to determine what you offer, what you have to sell, and then to find those who will pay you for that. But first you need to understand *their* perspective and *their* needs.

## THE HIRING PROCESS

You've put a lot of time and work into making your resume look perfect. But to an employer who doesn't know you, your resume is another piece of paper from a stranger, and they don't have the bandwidth to go through all them. Imagine yourself in the employer's place:

Let's say John has received five hundred resumes for a mid-level manager position. It takes hours for him to go through them, even if he spends only ten seconds on each one, which is the estimated average time one spends looking at a resume. He scans the resumes, looking for something that will eliminate each one—a typo, an out-of-city applicant, an overqualified applicant, et cetera. Finally he has culled his stack of resumes down to ten seemingly qualified candidates. The next step is to arrange a phone interview with each, after which five of the ten have been eliminated. Now it's time to bring in those five for face-to-face interviews, after which two more have been eliminated. The three remaining applicants have submitted three references each, which means nine phone calls that John needs to make. And what does John learn from each of these people? That their candidate is wonderful.

Next John has to bring the three candidates back in to meet with key members of his team. (Are you exhausted yet? Imagine how John is feeling.) Then comes a follow-up meeting with his team members to get their input. Perhaps in that meeting, one of the three candidates is eliminated. Now John must bring in the two finalists, interview them again, choose one, and make an offer. Let's say John extends an offer to Fred.

Fred starts work a couple of weeks later, and three weeks after that, the consensus among the team is that Fred isn't working out. Perhaps he misrepresented himself. Now John has to face Bill, his boss. Naturally Bill expresses his disappointment that over several months and five hundred resumes, Fred was the best John could come up with. Now Bill might reconsider giving John that promotion.

The whole previous scenario is overwhelming, and John decides not to go there. It's not worth the time or the risk. So what does he do? He doesn't even post the job. Instead he contacts his network of friends and colleagues to find someone to fill the position. These are people he trusts who have pre-screened the applicants, and John needs to minimize his risk. He doesn't want to hire a stranger who may not work out because his *own* job is at stake.

Lawrence W. Kellner, the Chairman and Chief Executive of Continental Airlines said this about his hiring tactics, "...Step one is...have I worked with somebody who could fill this job who's really good?... My success rate is dramatically higher going that route. If not, the second step is to widen the net to people who I trust, and look for people they've worked with..."

This is how business is done. It's said that 80 percent of jobs are never posted. Now you no longer have to wonder why.

## WHAT EMPLOYERS ARE LOOKING FOR

- A "service" attitude that's focused on *their* needs. Before you interview, research the company and be prepared to tell them specifically how you can fill those needs and why you are the solution to the problems they're having.
- A good fit. The truth is, employers don't always hire the most qualified person for the job. They hire the person who fits on the team.
- Someone who's easy to get along with, someone your co-workers can enjoy being around for hours at a time.
- A distinct impression. You stand out from the crowd.
- People who hustle. When all of the above are relatively equal, an employer will hire the person who is "hungry" and does the extra preparation/work to prove it.

Hustle can mean researching your interviewer. Yokesh was a student of mine at Pepperdine University. He had been asked to interview for a position with a big financial firm and came to me for coaching. We visited the firm's website and found a short bio about Bob, the executive Yokesh was to interview with. The bio spoke of Bob's involvement in a charity for Wilson's Syndrome. I advised Yokesh to do some research and ask Bob about his interest in it during their interview.

Yokesh followed my coaching and, toward the end of his interview, he asked Bob about Wilson's Syndrome. Bob told Yokesh that he was the first person out of twelve candidates he'd interviewed who had asked him about it, and he gave him the job on the spot! To Bob, Yokesh's question showed he had done his homework and was willing to do extra work to get the job.

# CHAPTER FOUR

# COMMUNICATION

*There is no magic, only brute persistence,*
*consistency, and attention to detail.*
*–Tom Peters*


*Decide what you want and decide what you are*
*willing to exchange to get it,*
*establish your priorities and get to work.*
*–H.L. Hunt*


You need a degree, an error-free resume, and a strong cover letter…and they may not even get you an interview! Those may have worked in the twentieth century, but they're no longer enough. What else do you need today? You need to develop your "brand."

Once you have a sense of your brand, you can develop your USP—your Unique Selling Proposition, a marketing term that distinguishes how people perceive one brand from another. All brands have defining characteristics—whether it's Coke, Pepsi, or *you*, selling your own skill set and experience—and those characteristics may be real or perceived. As we know, sometimes perception *is* reality.

I train my clients to determine, articulate, and sell their brand. It takes time to develop any skill, including the skills you'll need to find work, which is why it's called *training*. Figuring out what it is you offer in the workplace and how you promote that does not come naturally to most people. In fact, it's usually a struggle at the beginning. People do what they do, whether it's being a chemist, a graphic designer, or a financial analyst, and then I ask them to *sell* that.

It takes time and practice to learn to package and market yourself when all you really want to do is practice your vocation or, to put it another way, to do what you were meant to do.

Think of anything you do well, whether it's riding a bike, drawing, cooking, dancing— you name it. You do it better now than you did it the first time you tried it. Why? Because it's all a *process*. As the American composer Philip Glass has said, "You practice and you get better. It's very simple." So it is with the practice of selling yourself.

I tell my clients that I have no commitment to their *enjoyment* of selling themselves. They are developing a new habit, like brushing one's teeth. I wouldn't tell a client, "Guess what! Tonight you get to go home and brush your teeth! Doesn't that sound like fun?" Their answer would no doubt be along the lines of, "Are you crazy? That's not fun. It's a habit." What I do with my clients is train them to develop another habit—selling themselves—something they'll be doing for as long as they work.

A few years ago I was visiting my fiancée (now my wife) in Manhattan over the Christmas holidays. She had two dogs and of course we had to walk them every morning. The weather that winter was particularly cold, even for New York. I'm not a fan of cold weather, but I bundled myself up in layers and, at 6:00 a.m. and half asleep, we walked over to what New Yorkers call a "dog run"—actually a slab of pavement surrounded by a fence. I was freezing and it was the last place I wanted to be.

My fiancée introduced me to the only other dog owner at the run, Laura Morrison. Laura was writing a piece for the Wall Street Journal's Career Journal. Freezing and sleepy at a dog park at 6:00 a.m.—the unlikeliest of places to network—I immediately went into networking mode. I told Laura what I did, we exchanged business cards, and she later quoted me in her article. My advice to you is to always carry your business card and always be prepared to network, no matter where you are or what time it is.

## BRAND - AND MARKETING YOURSELF

A brand is a relationship; what does your market think and feel about you and your skills, abilities, and experience? What's your reputation?

When you think of Coke, what comes to mind?

- Brown
- Bubbly
- Sweet
- Refreshing
- Caffeine kick
- Carbonated

When your market thinks of you, what comes to mind?

- Creative
- Follow-through
- Friendly
- Team player
- Hardworking
- Quick learner
- Good attitude

Or is it:

- Flaky
- Drama queen
- Difficult
- Excuses
- Unreliable

Your brand is a list of three or four specific marketable and transferable skills you can monetize. What I'm talking about are *hard* skills, like the languages you speak, the software programs you're proficient with, the quantifiable results you've attained for other companies. In other words, what distinguishes you? What makes you stand out from the competition? What's makes your brand unique? As an employer who may be willing to pay you, what exactly are you going to be able to do for *me*?

I stress *specific* skills because I've seen far too many resumes listing skills like "good team player," "able to work independently," "good oral and written communication skills." These are too general, and they're a given for someone who has a degree.

Let's work on how to state your attributes. For example:

- Fluent in Spanish, Mandarin, and English.

Fluent means you can speak, read, and write in the language. *Business fluent,* as I describe it, means that if an employer hires you and puts you on the phone with a client in Shanghai, you know Mandarin well enough to close the deal.

- Proficient in Abode Illustrator and Photoshop, and QuickBooks.

Add whatever software is specific to the field in which you work—or the field in which you want to work. The first programs you list should be those of most value to the people in that field. Microsoft Office should come last, because you're *supposed* to know it and almost everyone does. Use "proficient" instead of "knowledgeable," as the employer is not interested in what you *know* but in what you can *do* for the company.

- Produced at least a 10 percent annual increase in sales for the last two companies for which I worked.

Provide quantifiable results. Numbers. In other words, what specifically did you *accomplish* and how did it impact the bottom line?

The combination of skills, experience, and performance you offer is unique in the world. I have worked with hundreds of people over the years and have yet to find two who were exactly alike.

Your brand—your reputation—always precedes you, and when you're being considered for work, it's what people think, remember, and say about you that determines whether you'll get a meeting.

While I was working with a film production company, the producer, Jim and the director, Debbie were talking about editors they might want to work with, when Ralph's name came up. Their conversation about him was brief:

- Jim: What about Ralph for the editor's job?
- Debbie: No. He's a pain in the ass.

Often it's unconscious, but the people who meet you, spend time with you, work with you—your family members, friends, and coworkers—are always cataloguing your behaviors. While friends and family are more forgiving, the impression you make determines how willing others will be to put in a good word for you, recommend you, or provide you with a lead in the future.

You should make sure that anyone you spend time with has a good feeling about you. They won't stick their necks out for someone who may embarrass them to a business associate and close off that relationship for themselves. Like it or not, you're always on display, always auditioning, and must always be "on."

## WRITING RESUMES: A NEW APPROACH

A resume is a *marketing* document designed to interest potential employers in your relevant skills and accomplishments. A resume is the script for telling your professional life story. Like makeup, it needs to accentuate your best features while hiding your flaws. Employers or clients are not interested in everything you've done, just in what you've done that's relevant to their needs.

I played the drums for fifteen years, but that fact doesn't appear anywhere on my resume unless I'm applying for a job teaching music. You don't have to disclose everything you've ever done. Go to confession if you feel the urge.

You should never lie on a resume, but your objective is to fill the needs of the employer, and given they only care about *their* needs, your resume should address and be customized for that.

Below is an example of a resume before, and after I worked on it with the student. Personal information has been changed to protect the innocent.

BEFORE . . .

### Paul Irviz

Home: (818)601-9417               Address: 130 mann Ave#21
Cell: (818)434-2111                 Van Nuys, CA 91423
E-mail: irviz621@yahoo.com

Objective: To obtain a challenging accounting position, where I can utilize my years of experience and knowledge.

Experience:
**5/2007–present          GFI Industries Inc          Pasadena CA
Accounting Manager**
- Responsible for account reconciliations and general maintenance to insure proper posting account and to the correct accounting periods.
- Manage and control A/P and A/R
- File sales tax for more than 40 states every month.
- Allocated payroll to the job cost
- Assists the CFO with special projects.
- Control petty cash.
- Worked closely with HR.

**6/2001–4/2007      Big Time Chevrolet Body Shop   VanNuysCA**
**Accountant**
- Responsible for General Ledger, A/R, A/P, Bank reconciliation.

34

- Cost Accounting.
- Payroll.
- Processing invoices.
- Involve with customer service and insurance companies.

**8/2000–5/2001      Tom's Trucking Co          Northridge CA**
**Accountant**
- A/P, A/R
- Banks reconciliation

**5/1999–8/2000      Ernst & Young Co              Egypt**
**Accounting System Analyst: (assigned to various large accounting projects)**
- **Project: EgyptMotors**: (The largest car manufactures in Egypt, with 50,000 employees) Designed general accounting system, cost accounting system, and inventory system. Studied and researched accounting critical points and rendering proposition in car manufacturing.
- **Project: Gas Company**: Designed cost accounting, inventory, and purchases system for entire company.

**5/1997–5/1999      Mobar (accounting Egypt**
                     **consultative company)**
**Accounting System Designer: (assigned to various large accounting projects)**
- **Project: Achmed Farm (Chicken Farm):** Designed general accounting system, cost accounting system, inventory system, accounts payable and accounts receivable system

- **Project: Recration and Sport Company:** Designed General accounting, Cost accounting, Accounts Payable and Receivable Systems
- **Project: Egyptian Fishery Company:** Designed General and Cost accounting systems, Petty cash and Inventory Systems

**6/1995–6-1997**      **Telefund Cable Company**      **Egypt**
**Accounting Manager**
- Responsible for account reconciliations and general maintenance to insure proper posting account and to the correct accounting periods
- Manage and control A/P and A/R
- Control fixed assets

**3/1989–6/1994**      **Amero Chemical Company**      **Egypt**
**Accounting Manager**
- Responsible for account reconciliations and general maintenance to insure proper posting account and to the correct accounting periods
- Manage and control A/P and A/R
- Control fixed assets
- Cost accounting

**Education**
- 1991 Cairo university B.A. Accounting
- 2005 Los Angeles Valley College A.A Economics
- 2009 Attending Pepperdine University for MBA program

**Special Skills**
- Over 250 hours of training in accounting system design by Ernst & Young CO
- MAS 90 Accounting Software
- Microsoft Business Navision Software
- Quick Books Software
- Microsoft Office (Excel, Word, Power Point)

# Reference
- Mark Cooper CPA Mobar's CFO (818)421-1210
- David Baum  Mobar's HR (719)645-1423
- Harve Big Time Chevrolet Bodyshop Owner (818)475-3621
- Chery Vicko  Big Time Chevrolet CFO (818)475-3621
- Harold Garvin  CPA Firm Partner (949)412-1128


AFTER . . .

### PAUL IRVIZ
### CONTROLLER
130 Mann Avenue #21, Van Nuys, CA 91423
Home: (818) 601-9417, Cell: (818) 434-2111, irviz621@yahoo.com


### EXPERIENCE

**ACCOUNTING MANAGER,**

GFI Industries, Inc., Pasadena, CA                     5/2007 – present
*Manage and control A/P, A/R, and petty cash. File sales tax for more than 40 states every month.*
*Allocate payroll to job costs. Responsible for account reconciliations and general maintenance.*
*Assist the CFO with special projects. Work closely with HR.*


**ACCOUNTANT,**

Big Time Chevrolet Body Shop, Van Nuys, CA       6/2001 – 4/2007
*Responsible for General Ledger, A/R, A/P, bank reconciliations, cost accounting, payroll,*
*and processing invoices. Involved with customer service and insurance companies.*


**ACCOUNTANT,**

Tom's Trucking Co., Northridge, CA                     8/2000 – 5/2001
*A/P, A/R, and bank reconciliations.*


**ACCOUNTING SYSTEM ANALYST** assigned to large accounting projects
Ernst & Young Co., Egypt                               5/1999 – 8/2000
***EgyptMotors****: (Egypt's #1 car manufacturer, with 50,000 employees): Designed general accounting, cost accounting, and inventory systems. Researched accounting critical points and rendering proposition in car manufacturing.*

*Gas Company: Designed cost accounting, inventory, and purchasing systems for the entire company.*
Over 250 hours of training in accounting system design.

**ACCOUNTING SYSTEM DESIGNER** assigned to large accounting projects
*Mobar* (accounting consultative company), Egypt      5/1997 – 5/1999
*Achmed Chicken Farm: Designed general accounting, cost accounting, inventory, A/P, and A/R systems.*

*Recreation and Sports Company: Designed general accounting, cost accounting, A/P, and A/R systems.*
*Egyptian Fishery Company: Designed general and cost accounting, petty cash, and inventory systems.*

**ACCOUNTING MANAGER,**
Telefund Cable Company, Egypt      6/1995 – 6/1997
*Managed and controlled A/P and A/R. Controlled fixed assets. Responsible for account reconciliations*
*and general maintenance.*

**ACCOUNTING MANAGER,**
Amero Chemical Company, Egypt      3/1989 – 6/1994
*Cost accounting. Managed and controlled A/P and A/R. Controlled fixed assets.*
*Responsible for account reconciliations and general maintenance.*

## EDUCATION

**M.B.A.**, Pepperdine University      2010
**A.A. in Economics**, Los Angeles Valley College      2005
**B.A. in Accounting**, Cairo University      1991

## SOFTWARE

MAS 90 Accounting, Microsoft Business Navision Software, QuickBooks, Microsoft Office

Let's analyze the changes I made—and why I made them. Less is always more in business writing (and speaking), so my first question was: is it possible to compress this resume to one page?

There is a constant argument about whether a resume should be one or two pages long. If you can, learn the preference of the employer you're pursuing. Some are adamantly opposed to resumes longer than one page. If this is the case, compress your resume to one page. If the employer doesn't care, it doesn't matter.

If you have less than ten years' experience, a one-page resume is probably sufficient. The editing process will be useful because you'll learn what is it you've accomplished that really matters and that you can deliver to your next employer. If, after paring it down, you still have a page and a half, keep working at it until it's one page. Get someone else to look at it; a fresh set of eyes can spot redundancies or a lack of clarity in your text and layout.

I compressed Paul's contact information to two lines and gave him a brand: Controller. This allowed me to remove his objective. There's no right answer about whether to include an objective in a resume. Frankly, it depends on what's in fashion. Of course, you can avoid the issue altogether by finding the "side door" to the employer—if they already know you, whether or not you have an objective won't matter.

Now to the question of where to put your education. As with a sound bite, you lead with what's strongest. If you have a lot of experience, put it first. If you don't, begin with your education.

On Paul's resume, I removed all the bullets and condensed the descriptions for three reasons: (1) to save space, (2) because English is obviously not Paul's first language, and (3) because fewer words have more impact. Paul would do well to memorize the key action verbs in his resume in order to sell himself in an interview. Employers appreciate action verbs like managed, controlled, allocated, designed, and researched.

I also eliminated the references, because references do not belong on a resume. They should be on a separate sheet of paper and presented when the interviewer asks for them. Having this ready will show that you are prepared.

## WRITING COVER LETTERS: A HOW-TO

Read the job description carefully. Are you really a fit? I like to have my clients print out the job description and go over it word for word. It's surprising how often people overlook the obvious and see what they want to see instead of what's actually written.

One client wanted to work for Google, but the job description clearly stated that they needed someone with a lot of technology experience, and she had virtually none. It was difficult for her to hear that Google was not likely to consider her, but she finally accepted that she would need to look elsewhere for a company that would embrace the skills she did have.

Once you've determined that you are a good fit, it's time to write. Your cover letter should consist of three paragraphs:

**1. The Connection**. Get the reader's attention. Remember, they're busy. The first thing they want to know is why you're writing them. What job are you interested in? Are you answering a posting? Where did you find the posting? Were you referred by a mutual contact? If so, mention that contact's name in the first sentence or, if it's an e-mailed cover letter, in the subject line. For example: "Dan Jones suggested I contact you."

**2. The Match**. Go through the job description and highlight the specific requirements they want. Write about the top three or four. You can even use bullets. For example:
- Your job description asks for at least three years of product management experience, and I have five.
- You require an M.B.A. in finance, and I hold an M.B.A. in finance from [name of your university].
- You need someone who is proficient in both Quicken and QuickBooks, and I have taught courses in both programs at my local community college for the past four years.

**3. The Next Step**. It's not business unless it's a calendar item with a specific date and time. Otherwise, it's just bar talk. "Hey, baby,

I'll call ya soon." When exactly is soon? Tomorrow? Next week? Next month? Add something like, "I look forward to meeting with you in person on Thursday at noon."

The trouble is, the percentage of people who get interviews by sending a resume to a stranger is extremely low, and that's why cover letters are not of dire importance. If you've heeded my advice, you'll already know the person, and a cover letter may not be necessary.

## THE PITCH

The next step is to refine and polish your pitch. Your pitch—also known as your sound bite, or elevator pitch—is your succinct answer to the question people ask when they meet you: "What do you do?" People need a shorthand way to categorize you for their mental Rolodex, so your pitch tells them where you fit. Your pitch is your primary sales tool, and you'll be using it for the rest of your life. It will change over time as your experience and skills grow and your goals change, and depending on to whom you're speaking.

The points I hit in my own pitch are that I am a career mentor, author, and college professor.

The order in which I place the elements in my pitch depends upon who my audience is. For example, if I'm talking to a publisher, it's some version of, "Hello, I'm Chaz Austin (or Dr. Austin, or Dr. Chaz—whichever is appropriate). I'm an author, career mentor, and college professor." Notice that "author" comes first. The trick is learning to whom you're speaking. Let the other person talk first, if possible. Then you'll have a better idea of what to tell them about yourself—what will interest them about you, from a business perspective. Your pitch can even change at the same networking event.

But, you may say, it's misrepresenting yourself or even lying to change your pitch to suit the audience. What if you spend more time as a career mentor than as an author? Shouldn't you be honest and talk first about what you do the most?

To that I say let's go back to what this is all about. While it's true that you are promoting yourself, what's important are the needs of the people you meet. What's of interest to a publisher? Obviously, that I'm an author. Whatever else I do may not be of much interest to them at all.

Below is a client's original pitch for an internship she was seeking:

> Hello. I am currently looking for internships within the finance industry during summer. As you know, I am enrolled in the State University MBA program. I received my under-graduate degree in finance and French and I am also fluent in Farsi. I would greatly appreciate it if you could see if any positions are available for me through your connections.

The client and I revised and shortened her pitch to:

> I need an internship in finance this summer. I earned my BS in finance and French from Northern Cal and am cur-rently in the MBA program at State University. I'm also fluent in Farsi. Can you refer me to people you know?

No matter how much my clients may dislike having to sell themselves, I train them to get comfortable being articulate with their pitch. So comfortable that if I call them at 3:00 a.m. and wake them from a sound sleep, they can easily tell me what it is they do. You need to be able to do the same. Yes, you are selling yourself. You're selling *you, the brand.*

Again, you don't have to *enjoy* doing this. You don't even have to be great at it, just good enough so people know what you offer and can refer or hire you for work.

You may not be the very best at what you do, but you'll get the work because you were known by the hiring manager and his or her trusted associates, you were available, and you were good enough to do the job.

# HOW TO INTERVIEW (INCLUDING QUESTIONS THEY'LL ASK YOU)

Interviewing should be rehearsed over and over again so you, the candidate, become comfortable fielding answers to the typical questions in a formal interview. Following are some of those questions, and guidelines on how to answer them.

- Tell me about yourself. What adjectives would you or your friends use to describe you?

It's important to note that before answering this question, it is useful to get clarification before proceeding with an answer. In this case, you might ask, "What specifically in my resume stood out that you would like me to talk about?" This will help you to direct the interview, and after the employer answers the question, you will be able to focus your answer on what he or she is looking for.

- What got you interested in what you do? Why did you choose to do what you do? What makes a good candidate for this job?
- What are your greatest strengths?

Remember, this is a business meeting. Your interviewer is interested in strengths that are applicable to their bottom line. *Their* needs come first. So being an "excellent windsurfer" is probably not what you should talk about. Instead, mention things like your ability to generate new business, your hard work ethic, and your creativity in finding solutions that aren't apparent at first glance.

- What do you consider your greatest accomplishment?

Provide an answer that applies to your career. If you don't have a lot of work experience, talk about your accomplishments in school. If you've raised children—your own or your siblings—you can use that. Some of the best office managers are women (or men) who've returned to the workforce after raising their families, and a hiring manager will appreciate that you can easily deal with the "children" in the office.

- What is your biggest weakness? Name two things you'd like to improve about yourself.

People are invariably perplexed about how to answer this question. They want to be honest but don't want to expose any weakness. It seems that in interviews, there is the answer to the question you're being asked, and then there's the *real* answer they're looking for. They seem to be asking you to make yourself vulnerable by confessing a shortcoming. What they actually want to know is: *have you learned to manage yourself?*

Dale Chapman, a very wise coach I had, once said that no one gets rid of their bad habits; we just learn to manage them. Thus, the way to answer this question is to state the "weakness" ("I'm a workaholic"), and then how you've learned to handle it. ("What I've learned is that after twelve or fourteen hours, I run out of steam; so I quit for the day, get a good night's sleep, and am ready to go full steam ahead the next morning.")

This tells the interviewer three things: (1) You're self-reflective and honest about your limitations. (2) You're a workaholic. This is a *good* thing in the business world. Have you ever noticed that employers will pay for programs to help you with alcoholism, cocaine abuse, and anger management, but there are no programs to wean you off of working too hard? (3) You're a *managed* workaholic. You've learned to successfully deal with problems. The assumption is that if you can manage yourself, you may be able to manage others. Companies like to spot potential management talent and hire people who can move up in the ranks.

- How do your co-workers and friends describe you? What would they say you need to improve?

This is another version of the preceding question, only this time you also get to say some positive things about yourself.

- Are you a team player? Give me some examples.

Your answer should include how you put the team's needs above your own.

- Describe a time when you worked with someone "difficult." What happened, and how did you resolve the problem?

Use the following template to answer this question: (1) Outline what happened. (2) Describe how you took action. (3) Explain the result, which should be some *improvement.*

- Why did you leave your last job (or, why are you leaving your current job)?

NOTE: Don't trash your last employer. In fact, never say anything bad about anyone. It may well come back to bite you and, at the very least, make you look like a whiner or a victim. No one wants to be around that kind of person.

- What would you like to be doing a year, five years, ten years from now?

If you're young, you may not have any idea. Remember, you're not under oath, so you don't have to commit to what you say. What they really want to know is if you're ambitious and forward-thinking, so your answer could be something like, "I see myself becoming the CEO of this company or one like it," or, "Someday I'd like to run my own business in this industry."

- If you were an animal, what animal would you be?

Yes, they really ask this question, and they do it to throw you off balance. In class, a male student once answered honestly, "A soft pussycat." Try to match the animal to the kind of job for which you're applying. For a sales job, they want someone who's quick and aggressive, like a cheetah or a shark. For a senior management position, perhaps you'd be an elephant or a lion.

- If you were part of a salad, what part would you be? (Variations include: If you could be any superhero, who would you be, and why? What color best represents your personality?)

Same type of answer as the previous question. (Are you beginning to understand why it's easier to know people so you can avoid the formal interview and these sorts of silly questions?)

Now that you've got some practice giving answers your potential employer wants to hear, try your hand at these:

- What new skills have you recently developed?
- How do you handle deadlines?
- How do you balance your priorities?
- How do you deal with criticism?
- How do you deal with stress?
- Give me an example of a time you failed.
- Give me an example of a time you showed leadership.
- Why should we hire you? What unique qualities or abilities would you bring to this job that would make you successful?
- Give me an example of a time you had to be creative to solve a problem at work.
- Give me an example of a time you persuaded or influenced a group of people.
- Tell me about your most difficult boss. How was he or she difficult? How did you deal with him or her?
- Why is there a gap in your resume?
- How does your previous experience relate to this position?
- Why do you want to work here? What do you know about this company?
- Tell me about your experience at your college or university. Why did
- you choose to attend that school?

46

- What was your favorite class in school, and why? Your most challenging class, and why?
- What are you passionate about?
- Tell me about one of your most creative moments, either professional or personal.
- What are the most rewarding aspects of a job for you?
- What successful people in your field inspire you, and why?
- Sell me on my company or product.
- What are your pet peeves?
- What does success mean to you?
- If you felt any weakness pertaining to this job, what would it be?
- What has been your biggest career-related crisis?
- What are the things that motivate you?
- Describe your ideal job.
- At what point did you choose this career?
- What motivates you to put forth your greatest effort?
- Give examples of your experiences at school or in a job that were satisfying. Dissatisfying?
- Provide examples to convince me that you can adapt to a wide variety of people, situations, and environments.
- Tell me about a time you had to juggle multiple responsibilities. How did you organize the work?
- Tel me about a time you had to make a decision, but didn't have all the information you needed.
- Give an example of something you did to build enthusiasm in others.
- Give an example of a time someone you worked with criticized you in front of others. What was your response?
- Give an example of a time you had to sell a supervisor on a concept or idea. What steps did you take? Did you win?

## QUESTIONS YOU CAN (AND SHOULD) ASK THEM

Remember that in an interview, part of your job is to learn if the potential employer is a good fit for *you*. To use a dating analogy: just because someone asks you out, doesn't mean you have to say yes. First you'd ask a few questions to determine whether you're compatible. Why should choosing an employer be any different? An interview is a *conversation*—one that happens to be about business. You don't need to act desperate, because the employer may want you, too; it will be your job to let the employer know *why* that is so.

It's important that you have confidence in what you offer to the marketplace. The better you feel about yourself, the greater your self-worth, and the easier it will be for you to question the employer. Your mindset should be that the employer has to be good enough for you. Now that you've built the foundation that connects you to your passions and marketability and are comfortable with selling yourself, the time has come for the employer to sell himself to *you*.

To properly prepare for the interview, you will want to research the organization with which you'll be interviewing, including:

- Visiting LexisNexis and/or Hoovers.com for financial data.
- Finding news articles about the company's activities, possible negative press, pending lawsuits, product recalls, and the like.
- Researching any personal contacts in your database who may know the inside story of what's going on in the company.
- Scouring the company's website, the good face on who they are and what they do.

After your due diligence has been completed, it is appropriate to ask them any further questions you have to determine whether they are a suitable organization for you. Acceptable questions include:

- How long have you worked here, and how do you like it?

- How many people have left your department in the past year or two (or since you began your employment with this organization)? Why did they leave?
- What types of training programs does the company offer?
- If you hired me, what would my typical day look like?
- What metrics would be used to evaluate my performance on the job?

It's important that your potential for keeping your job or getting a raise or a promotion is based on more than your boss's "gut feeling" about you. If you've hit or exceeded your targets, it's harder for them to wriggle out of delivering what they promised.

- What's the worst thing about working here?

Don't expect an honest answer. Pay attention to how they deal with what will be a surprising question. If they tell you "nothing," be very suspicious. No job is perfect, and you want to know as much as you can about the bad stuff so you can determine whether you can live with it.

- Why should I pick your firm over your competitors?
- If you could do any one thing to improve your working conditions, what would it be?
- What, in *your* mind, is the mission of this company, and is it being realized? If not, why not?
- Describe the company culture.
- What's your management style? If I asked the people who work for you how supportive and inspiring you are, what would they say?

Again, like dating, it's important to show that you're interested in the employer. Beyond talking about the company and your suitability for the position, you should be knowledgeable and prepared to discuss trends in the particular industry in which the company operates.

# CHAPTER FIVE

# NETWORKING

*Let me tell you the secret that has led me to my goal.*
*My strength lies solely in my tenacity.*
*–Louis Pasteur*


*Everybody wants to go to heaven, but*
*nobody wants to die.*
*–Unknown*


*No great thing is created suddenly.*
*–Epictetus*


## THE GRANULAR DATABASE

The foundation of networking is the creation of a granular database. Your granular database should be both electronic and portable, residing in whatever device you carry around at all times—your smartphone, iPad, or laptop—because you never know when and where you'll need to connect with someone, and you'll want your database accessible.

The traditional database—it used to be called a Rolodex—contained the names of contacts and their phone numbers and addresses. A *granular* database includes these and so much more:

- Places they've lived
- Places they've worked, including their job titles
- Names of their significant others, children, and pets
- Important dates in their life (birthdays, anniversaries, etc.)
- Their hobbies and interests
- Personality traits and quirks, pet peeves and behaviors—what I call "sweet spots." These may include things like: loves scotch, very sarcastic, practical joker, hates libertarians, Anglophile, et cetera.

You're building a detailed profile of everyone you know. You may be asking how you're supposed to get all this personal information. Do you pretend you're a reporter or a police detective and give the people you meet the third degree? Not at all. As you spend time with people and break bread and get to know them, they'll talk about themselves. When the meeting's done, you make notes about whatever you can remember they said. You enter that in your database, and over time you'll fill in all the fields above.

You do all this work so you'll have reasons to stay in touch that are about *them*, not *you*. You don't want to have to contact someone you know to ask them if they have a job for you or know where you can find work. That often makes people uncomfortable because they can't help you, or feel you're annoying them. Or it may remind them that their own job may not be all that secure.

Instead, your granular database, which you program to alert you to significant events in the lives of your contacts, gives you reasons to stay on their radar by contacting them to talk about themselves and their lives. And who are people most interested in? Themselves, of course.

It's all about *access*.

When I was in sales, I had, as one of my bosses described it, "the tenacity of a bulldog on a pant leg." I would make a hundred phone calls a day, and from that, get a couple of appointments and one sale. Years later, when I became a Hollywood agent, I learned about access. Access is the ability to make *one* phone call to a decision-maker, close the sale, and spend the rest of the day at the beach. Smart employers are interested in the results, not the process. Employers and clients don't pat you on the back for the effort you made. It's about efficiency: how little work can you do to produce the desired results?

If you have your own business, your clients don't care how hard you work, either. They just want to know if you got them what they asked for, on time and on—or under—budget. It's *your* job to be efficient. The less time you spend on something, the higher your hourly rate. A time management mantra I've used for many years is, "does it cost me money or does it make me money?"

*It's not what you know. It's not even who you know. It's how well you know them and how often you appear on their radar.*

There is an old cartoon that captures networking very well. It shows two men having lunch together at a restaurant. The caption has one of the men saying to the other: Take my word for it. No Internet superhighway, I don't care how robust and sophisticated it may be, will ever replace "the art of the schmooze".

Your granular database is a tool you'll be able to update and use for the rest of your life to keep track of (and *schmooze*) the people you know. It is the key ingredient for organized and systematic networking. You will eventually have thousands of people you know and need to stay in touch with, and your granular database is what will allow you to do that.

## NETWORKING

I define networking as *making friends for the purpose of advancing your career.* Remember: companies don't hire you; people do.

Networking is about connecting with people in a way that brings benefit to both of you. Your orientation should shift to: how can I be *of service* and a *contribution* to others?

*When people are serving, life is no longer meaningless.* –*John Gardner*

Talin Koutnouyan, with whom I worked at Woodbury University, explained what a difference the service approach made for her: "After I shifted my way of thinking, I walked into every interview giving off the vibe that I was there to serve and exert all my effort for them. Today, I got a call telling me I had three offers from three different interviews. Not only that, but since all of the employers I had interviewed with were aware of the number of offers I had, I chose the position that best matched my skills and had the most competitive pay of the three."

I work with my clients to create and develop their narrative, their "story." Then I have them rehearse until they can comfortably articulate it. Only *then* do I have them move to networking.

Your audience is potential clients, employers, and people who can refer you. So, with your pitch in place, let's figure out who you are going to target and how you can find them and get them interested in who you are and what you have to sell.

So where do you start? You never know who might know someone in your field until you ask them, so begin with your family and friends, including the people who see you at weddings and tell you, "If there's anything you need, let me know."

Well, now you have something you need. No, it's not a job—not *yet*, anyway. What you need from those who love you are introductions to people who may be able to help advance your career.

See if you can get a meeting and begin to develop a relationship with a friend of a friend who has the potential to become a new colleague. The next part, finding work, will present itself later. Your new contact, the person to whom you've been introduced, knows why you're meeting. When you first meet, give them a good sense of what you can do and what you're looking for. Over time, they'll grow to know you, like you, and trust you, and they'll be happy to refer you for work.

Developing relationships is a long-term process. Trust is not built overnight or at one or two meetings. Would you refer someone for a job whom you had just met or hardly knew? Of course not. Think of yourself as a farmer. You plant the seeds—in this case, the seeds of a relationship—nurture them, and they grow over time.

When you get a no ("no, we're not going to hire you," "no, we're not going to interview you," "no, I don't know anyone I can introduce you to") it's useful to think of it as a "not yet." As Margaret Thatcher said, "You may have to fight a battle more than once to win it."

## AFFINITY GROUPS

You want to connect with anyone with whom you have something in common, as these are the people most likely to help you in your life and career. Human beings are tribal by nature, and people take care of their own.

Affinity groups can be related to: religion (members of your church), ethnicity (people of your ethnic heritage), geographic location (your neighbors), similar passions (fans of your favorite band or sports team), academia (members of your college alumni association, fraternity, or sorority), charity (people who contribute or volunteer for the organizations you do), or common interests (dog owners, golfers, bicyclists, joggers). What hobbies do you have and what places do you frequent? You have something in common with the people you see there regularly; you're all members of the same club, so to speak.

I was once a guest speaker in a course for graphic artists at Otis College of Art & Design in Los Angeles. The professor, Patty Kovic, had her own graphic design business and was the mother of twin daughters. She told us, "You wouldn't believe how many referrals I've gotten from other people with twins!" The other parents of twins felt a connection—an *affinity*—with Patty and were happy to refer work to her.

We all have multiple examples of groups of people with whom we share something in common. Think about it: you take your dog to a dog park and meet other dog owners, right? You have your dogs in common. If they know what you do for a living, they are apt to refer you because you're "one of them." You ride your bike or jog or play tennis with the same group of people every week. They know you—they're in your affinity group. Use it. These people are happy to help you, but you need to tell them what you do.

Many people think that social networking is the same as networking. It's a beginning, but nothing will ever replace face-to-face communication. People hire people they know and trust, and trust is developed by getting to know someone in person and over time. It's important to remember this line about social networking: *If you think the people you're 'friending' are really your friends, try asking them for a loan.*

Linda Hudson, the President and CEO of BAE Systems, Inc., said this in an interview in the New York Times: "Business school graduates come with a great theoretical knowledge about business. But...they have almost no people skills.... We give them all the book smarts, but we don't tend to give them the other skills that go along with business."

To hone the skills Hudson refers to, *always* take the meeting. You never know who can help you in your career, and though it may not result in a new client or job, if you can't make a sale, make a friend. It's a slow seduction; you're getting people to fall in love with you professionally. As a culture, we've been watching movies for over a hundred years because we all love a good story; so I have my clients practice telling interesting stories about themselves in an engaging way. In the stories you tell, you become the hero of your own life. After all, everyone loves a hero.

# CHAPTER SIX

# BUDGETING

Given we're all freelancers in the twenty-first century—kind of like free agents in professional sports—it's essential that we treat ourselves as the business that we are. We all need to become conscious about money: what you're bringing in versus what you're spending. Speaking of what you're bringing in, if you're lucky enough to have a job, be aware of the difference between gross and net: when you earn a paycheck, you take home (net) roughly 70 percent of the gross.

Our collective inability to plan sufficiently has resulted in us not knowing "how to budget for our households or how to balance our checkbooks.... Shoppers who ignored the fine print on credit card agreements helped push consumer bankruptcies up 40%, to 801,840, in 2007. The average college student graduates with $2,200 in credit card debt and is more likely to drop out of school because of financial hardship than because of academic failure." *Increasing Financial Literacy: What You Don't Know Can Hurt You* (Copyright January 27, 2008. Los Angeles Times. Reprinted with Permission).

As I said earlier, there are two ways to make money: increase revenue, and cut expenses. As expenses go, we must look at the cost versus the benefit, which can be difficult to decide. For example, do you attend a networking meeting or stay home and e-mail your client base to learn if they have any upcoming work for you? In this case, it may be a crapshoot: you might attend the meeting and find it was a waste of time and you would have been better off staying home. Then again, you might go to the meeting and make a contact that changes your life. You'll never know unless you go.

Sometimes you can make yourself crazy with these worries. Just know that inevitably you will waste some of your time on meetings and proposals that yield no revenue, and that that's okay.

Focus on distinguishing *needs* from *wants*. Compare your business to the human body: when you get cold, notice how it's your extremities that get cold first. That's because your body heat is going toward protecting the vital organs. As the owner of your own business, your needs—your vital organs—include rent, utilities, car payment, food, and medicine. Some of what you think are needs (that latte every morning, expensive dinners, drinks with friends every Friday after work, concert tickets twice a month) are really wants. That becomes clear when it's between paying the rent or going out for dinner—you have no choice; you must do the responsible adult thing and postpone the extras.

You're serving as your own gas and brake. A car needs both, and you need to be both for your own life. Be the gas pedal to move things forward and the brake pedal so you don't crash.

The first rule of freelancing—and running your own business, for that matter—is to keep your overhead low. When developing your monthly budget, be aware of the following categories of expenses, and begin to always look for ways of trimming them.

- Education: tuition, books, and supplies

Can you buy books at half price, rent them, or borrow them from your classmates?

- Entertainment: eating out, cable, movies, concerts, theatre, sporting events, downloads, books, magazine subscriptions, vacations

How often do you go out? Can you cut back? Are you watching the premium channels you're paying for? Can you look for vacation deals?

- Food: groceries, lunches, snacks, alcohol

Can you shop somewhere less expensive? In bulk?

If you spend $10.00 per day for lunch five days a week, for forty-eight weeks a year, that's $2400 annually. If you buy lunch *one* day a week and bring your lunch for the remaining days, you will save $1920 annually.

Why are you drinking so much? It's not healthy. Some of us treat our cars better than we treat our own bodies. When are you going to start treating your body like a temple instead of an amusement park? (as Shirley said to Laverne).

- Grooming: clothing, makeup, hair, nails, laundry, dry cleaning

Can you buy at outlet stores? Are you addicted to designer labels? Can you have a friend do your hair? Maybe barter for something you can provide for them. Can you do your own nails rather than go to a salon?

- Health care: insurance, medication, gym membership

Is there a group insurance plan offered in your field that you can join? Would it be cheaper to buy weights and use them at home versus joining a gym?

- Housing: rent or mortgage, insurance, utilities, cell phone, texting, Internet, cleaning service/supplies

Can you get a roommate or move back in with your parents? Are your utility bills going up for reasons you don't understand? Call the company. You're spending how much for your cell phone? Can you get rid of the cleaning service and clean your own home?

- Transportation: car payment, gas, insurance, maintenance, repairs, parking, registration, bus pass

Is it time to get a cheaper car? Can you really afford the Mercedes?

- Other: pets, credit card payments, interest, loans, cigarettes, birthday gifts

Consolidate your credit cards, if possible. Why are you still smoking? It's expensive.

Are you saving any money? Create a cushion for birthday gifts and emergencies.

"We must learn to save and budget if we want to keep buying more stuff.... We must understand the concept of compound interest—how it hurts us when we pay only the minimum on our credit card bills. We must learn that low monthly payments don't equal affordability. We must be aware of the seductive power of marketing and separate our wants from our needs...that brokers, bankers, and salespeople aren't necessarily our friends. We must [also] understand that opening bank accounts and establishing credit are prerequisites to success in the twenty-first century." *Increasing Financial Literacy: What You Don't Know Can Hurt You* (Los Angeles Times. January 27, 2008)

Review your budget every six months and trim the waste or find new sources of revenue. If you have your own business, do that *every* month. Get conscious and start a new habit.


## THE MULTIPLE INCOME STREAMS APPROACH

If you ran a company, would you have just one client? Of course not. If for some reason the client went under, so would your company. To protect yourself, you have multiple clients. If you consider your freelance work your "business," then ideally you want multiple ways in which to generate income, all connected to and feeding off of one another.

I'll use myself as an example: I'm a career mentor. That's my brand. I can derive revenue for that brand in the following ways:

- Career counseling to individuals
- Teaching college courses in career development
- Leading workshops
- Leading seminars
- Consulting for colleges and universities
- Authoring articles and books
- Public speaking

This logic runs counterintuitive to the twentieth century idea of one job, one boss, one paycheck, but structuring your career in this way will help you survive and flourish in the new world of work.

# CHAPTER SEVEN

# NEGOTIATING

Whether it's for a salary, a raise, a car, or a home, negotiating is contextually rather simple. You should bear two numbers in mind: the amount you want, and the amount you're willing to settle for. Now that I've discussed budgeting, you know where you stand and are ready to negotiate.

Let's talk about negotiating a salary. You're going in for a second job interview and you know the subject of money will be addressed. The question is always: what do I ask for? The answer is: do your homework. Do your due diligence about the company you're interviewing with. Have some sense of how well they pay compared to their competitors. Research the industry to find out what the pay range is for the job for which you're applying. If you're going for a manager job, and the pay range is $48,000 to $55,000 annually, you *want* $55,000, of course. The real question is: how much do you *need?*

Unfortunately, there are no strict rules on how to navigate the negotiation process because every situation has its variables, like what package is being offered. There is more than just salary to consider; there are also benefits, vacation time, career opportunity, commute length, flex time, and so on.

Factoring in the above, know the amount your want—and the amount you can live with. An important rule of negotiating is to *be prepared to leave with nothing.* If you're living inside a budget, you won't be desperate to win and, in a negotiation, if you *must* close the deal, you've lost before you walk in the room. You have no freedom to turn the deal down if it makes no sense. Go in with your budget in mind, and don't take less than your lowest figure.

Good luck!

# CONCLUSION

*The business of the samurai consists in reflecting on his
own station in life, in discharging loyal service to his master if
he has one, in deepening his fidelity in associations with friends
and, with due consideration of his own position,
in devoting himself to duty above all.*
—Yamaga Soko

So what have we learned? *You* can decide. And you may not realize it for a while, because until you are ready to put these ideas into action, they may just dissolve in your mind as something interesting you once read. Only when you put these practices into action will they resonate for you and have an impact on the results you can achieve. Don't wait for a sign that says you're ready; create your own sense of urgency.

My hope is that these practices become behaviors for you and that you use them regularly until they become ingrained in you as muscle memory. These practices may not be fun, but they work to empower you to make your vocational dreams come true. Once you're doing that, everyone wins—you, the people you serve, and those who follow you. Someday *your* life could be an inspiration to others.

# PART TWO:

# TRAINING PROGRAM FOR STUDENTS IN HIGHER EDUCATION

*Give a man a fish and you feed him for a day.*
*Teach him how to fish and you feed him for a lifetime.*
*—Lao Tzu*

I teach people how to fish. I train my clients to identify their brand—and then how to sell it—to empower them to transition to the next phase of their lives.

But it is a *training,* and training for anything takes time. Adults who have been in the business world grasp the program's common-sense approach. This program really should begin on one's first day of college. Career development coursework should be integrated throughout a student's higher education, altering consciousness and creating practices that can be used for the rest of that student's life.

What follows is the design for the program.

# CHAPTER EIGHT

# LEVERAGING YOUR DEGREE

Whether you accept it or not, you will have many careers in your life. That's why worrying about finding the "right" job or career—especially when you get out of school—is a waste of effort. A wonderful concept to recognize is what Nicholas Bennison, a student of mine, called the "cumulative positive." It means that everything you do and learn will make you better at what you'll do next—that nothing is wasted. I've had many careers (and jobs) in my life: career counselor, writer/producer of promos for CBS and ABC, Hollywood talent agent, manager of the Temple City Kazoo Orchestra, video software salesman, video buyer, retail window display creator, Internet marketing and business developer, production and film and tape coordinator for Dick Clark Productions, offline video editor, and night desk clerk at the Hollywood Tropicana Motel. Every one of these positions have made me and continue to make me a better college professor and career mentor.

Your may feel that having earned a degree entitles you to a job. A degree is a great tool to have in your career, but it's not enough. And that next degree you may be planning to pursue is not the magic solution to your problems, no matter what the college recruiter may tell you. Experience always trumps your degree. It's necessary to look beyond your degree and ask *why* an employer would want to hire you. What combination of experience and specific skills do you offer that would impact his or her organization's bottom line?

Your degree is essential, and yet guarantees nothing. It's necessary but insufficient. I know, this one is tough to wrap your mind around, but a degree is not a silver bullet. "Then why bother?" you may ask. A degree is a valuable thing to have, but not for the reasons you may imagine.

Your degree gets you to the starting line. Some companies will not even consider you for a position without a degree, whether it's a BA, a BS, or an MBA. And you never know what benefit it might be to you later in life. My MA in Radio and Television helped me to get my first job in television—as a runner for Dick Clark Productions. "Runner" is a euphemism for delivery man, and with my master's degree, I earned $125 a week, and twenty-five cents a mile for every delivery. But I was part of the company, and within two weeks, I got a promotion, a big raise, and the two-week job stretched into eighteen months of work.

Your degree may provide unseen benefits. If you'd told me back then that what I was meant to do in this world was be a college professor, I would have told you that you were crazy. No way, no how was *that* ever going to happen. Little did I know that many years later, I would decide to pursue department chairs and find teaching positions in higher education. And without that MA, I would never have been considered for those positions.

But I was, and then I fell in love with teaching. Later, I began chafing at the limitations of being an adjunct professor, but universities wouldn't consider me for a staff position unless I had my doctorate. So, I got my doctorate! Does that mean that my door is being beaten down by every major university in southern California? Nope. But I've gotten myself to a new starting line and I can hustle and sell myself all over again.

You may now be asking, "Should *I* go back to school to get another degree?" I've seen many of my clients continue with their education and pursue yet another degree because they don't know what else to do or are afraid of going into—or *back* into—the workforce, particularly in a bad economy. Of course, there is no definitive answer, but generally I recommend you return to school to pursue another degree *after* you have work experience and if there's a definite purpose—such as recognizing a new passion—that justifies your time, effort, and the money you'll need to invest.

One of the main reasons people attend Ivy League schools is to gain access to people who have money and power: the decision-makers, the players, the movers and shakers. Some things to ask yourself are: is attending this school going to expand my options for the future? Will the people I meet and get to know be able to help me later in my life?

You will learn a lot in school, although you may not learn it in the classroom. A great deal of learning takes place in the periphery, and putting yourself in a stimulating environment and being open to new experiences will bring benefits you may not be aware of at the time, but that will prove useful later in life.

# CHAPTER NINE

# OVERVIEW OF THE PROGRAM

My colleagues in the business world regularly complain to me that college graduates:

- lack communication skills
- do not understand what relevant talents and experience they offer are not properly prepared with information about the businesses with which they interview and how they can make a contribution to those organizations
- are not properly prepared with information about the businesses with which they interview and how they can make a contribution to those organizations

For decades, college students have taken course after course after course to earn a degree, only to graduate without knowing what type of work they want to do. And if they did know, they were unequipped to find a job and instead spent years wandering the workplace without a clear sense of direction. Higher education has not been properly readying students for the working world.

It is time for higher education to radically alter the way it delivers career development. A career course program needs to be embedded into the standard college curriculum, because learning how to find work should be as important as any other subject studied in school. I work with my clients and students to "practicalize" their education—to *apply* what they've learned for the rest of their lives in all the careers they'll have. As Chekhov said, "Knowledge is of no value unless you put it into practice."

A student's education should be practicalized beginning during freshman year and continuing until graduation. Students should be trained over time via both one-on-one coaching sessions and required courses, as many of these skills are best learned in a group setting. For example: listening to students do a mock interview helps other students learn what works and what doesn't in an interview, whereas resumes need to be edited one-on-one. Career counselors can work with faculty to incorporate career instruction into the curriculum. Traditionally, these two functions have operated in separate silos.

According to a survey I conducted for my doctoral dissertation, the benefits of career development coursework (discussed in detail in the "Survey Results" section of this book) include:

- positive gains in students' preparedness for the workforce.
- positive impact on all genders and ethnicities of students.
- improvement in students' adjustment to college.
- decreased time until graduation, and improved GPAs.
- provided current information on the relative risks and rewards of different careers.
- better decision-making about graduate schools and careers.
- deeper understanding of the realities of the job market.
- more positive evaluations by employers.
- development of students support networks.
- greater job satisfaction.
- earlier career planning and increased career maturity.

Integrating a career development course program into a traditional curriculum can bridge the gulf between what businesses need in their employees, and graduates' readiness to fill those needs.

The most common response to my work has been: "Why didn't I take your courses sooner? If I knew all this when I went to college, I could have saved ten years in my career!"

In fact, eighty percent of the respondents to my survey agreed that career courses were valuable, and thirty percent of those respondents reported that, sadly, they themselves had had very little or no career preparation during college. Twenty percent believed that they were poorly prepared or not prepared at all for their current or most recent position, and it was not simply a matter of more courses or more time with a career counselor. Sixty-five percent of the survey subjects felt they were not even given a general, practical knowledge of how the workplace operates!

Woodbury University in Burbank, California, with whom I worked, was one of only thirty institutions in the United States to receive a College Success Awards Grant from the Council of Independent Colleges and the Walmart Foundation. The grant of $50,000 allows Woodbury to embed career coursework into the standard curriculum.

Beginning with their School of Business, career development courses will be integrated into each year of a student's studies. By emphasizing the skill sets necessary to succeed professionally, Woodbury's students will focus on how their studies will lead to their eventual careers. The grant will support career staff and business management faculty to develop the new career program, with the eventual goal of expanding it to encompass all majors within the university's other schools.

There is no reason why this type of program should not be part of the general curriculum of every college and university in the United States in the next decade.

After coaching hundreds of college and graduate students and individuals, and teaching career development courses for many years, it's clear to me that higher education needs an overhaul in the way we deliver career development. Rather than simple occasional one-on-one coaching sessions with a career counselor or a semester-long career development course near the end of college or graduate school, students should be trained over time to package and market themselves. While there are useful career courses offered at the college level, these are insufficient to the challenges facing people in the twenty-first century.

In present-day corporate America, the employment landscape includes layoffs, downsizing, offshoring, outsourcing, and mergers. Early retirement is increasingly being offered. With these prospects on the horizon, a college graduate has little alternative but to freelance.

Given the "new normal" of the working world, our role as educators is to properly prepare our students to navigate it. We need to "teach them what they have learned," build their self-confidence about who they have become during their years in school, help them define and market the specific skills they now can offer, and prepare them to be of service to employers.

## THE PROBLEM, AND WHY THE ISSUE IS IMPORTANT

There is a gap in higher education between how students are prepared to enter the workforce and what employers require in new employees. Students complain about not being properly taught how to find work, and employers complain that students do not have a firm sense of what it is they offer and how they can positively impact the needs of a business.

Because the traditional ways of preparing our students to enter the workforce are insufficient to the freelance workplace of the new century, as educators and career counselors, our mission must be to modernize and expand the manner in which we deliver career training.

In order for the United States to remain competitive, we also have to prepare our workforce for the global economy. Career training has traditionally focused on helping people acquire marketable skills. But as companies recruit, train, and promote from a worldwide labor pool, in addition to their skill set, American workers will need to develop a "global mindset," which will include understanding how to do business in and with other cultures and becoming fluent in more languages than just English, which brings me to this melancholy joke:

What do you call someone who knows two languages? Bilingual.

What do you call someone who knows three languages? Trilingual. What do you call someone who knows one language? American.

Students should be taught the skills required to find work and develop the flexibility to expand and adjust them to changing requirements. Just as any business owner is responsible for the growth of his or her company and its ability to adjust and flourish in a changing marketplace, students must be taught to take responsibility for the growth and development of their own careers.

This new world of work creates the opportunity for schools of higher education to transcend traditional forms of content delivery by preparing students for a world that requires both technical (hard) skills and communication (soft) skills. Career coursework needs to integrate vocational training into a traditional academic education. I'm prepared for resistance. The culture of colleges and universities has a built-in prejudice to what it sees as coursework belonging in a trade school. They've begrudgingly given office space to career counselors because their students and the parents of those students want some payback for their investment, but the counselors have been given no power.

With all these radical changes in the workplace, more needs to be offered to college students than a single career course or an optional hour-long meeting with a counselor. Training students how to market themselves is a process that can only be learned over time.

First we must understand the employer's perspective. Employers today are faced with a number of pressing issues:

*No time.* Technology, specifically laptops, iPads, and cell phones, have turned workers into their own secretaries and assistants. Workers in today's labor market are doing the work that in years past was performed by at least two people. Given their increased workload, employers and hiring managers do not have the time to conduct thorough searches of candidates to fill a particular job opening.

*Too many resumes.* Companies typically receive hundreds of resumes in response to any job posting and no longer have the time to read through all of them. They resort to their informal network of friends and colleagues to find appropriate candidates. Nobel laureate of 1957 Herbert Simon coined the term "satisficing," defined as the inclination to settle for the first solution that meets our minimum requirements. This is a necessary and pragmatic approach, especially whenever we face many choices. Thus the best candidates for a position are often never interviewed, and the person ultimately hired is someone (referred by a trusted colleague) who is simply "good enough" to do the job.

*Too much risk.* Given employers generally have no time to properly conduct due diligence on the people they interview, it is more prudent to rely on their own network of contacts. Job candidates referred by the people in this network will have been pre-screened by a friend or coworker.

Thus, the situation demands that jobseekers create a new strategy for finding work. What was successful in the twentieth century no longer applies, and we must adapt our teaching to this new environment. Career courses have proven effective, but students will be learning new habits and will need to complete a *series* of courses to develop them.

I believe that career development must become a mandatory part of the curriculum, where everything a student has learned is synthesized into an awareness of the talents and skills they have developed, and the student is then trained in how to sell that skill set to potential employers. I propose that this career curriculum be integrated into the general curriculum beginning during a student's freshman year of college, tying together all the other courses they have taken, replacing the traditional—and now obsolete—concepts of career preparation.

In the twentieth century, higher education consisted of a series of seemingly unconnected courses leading to a degree, and finding a job meant preparing and sending a resume and cover letter in response to a job opening and awaiting an invitation to interview. Career counseling consisted of an hour with a counselor, polishing a resume, and receiving job leads. Career counseling must be perceived and treated as more than a resume writing service or a job placement office in order impact our students' future success in the workplace.

The career development course program I propose addresses these problems, and my survey of professionals in the field endorses the need for such a program. We must train students to develop the skills they will need to continue to find work for the rest of their lives.

The program consists of three steps:

1. Make students aware of and able to *define* their personal brand and how the uniqueness of their skill set compares with other people competing for the same position.
2. Train students to *articulate* specifically what they have to sell to prospective employers or clients.
3. Strategize with students on how to *sell* their brand and how to find the people who can refer or hire them.

In other words: What am I selling? Who do I know? How can I help them?

Teaching students coping skills for the modern working world will meet with resistance. Few students are aware of or prepared to meet the challenges of a freelance marketplace where they will always need to be selling themselves. To begin to shift their consciousness and change their outlook, we need to dispel certain beliefs. Though their parents may have worked for one company until retirement, students can expect that they'll work for many companies, have multiple careers, and may never be able to afford to retire.

Their degree has become a commodity and will not guarantee them a job. According to the Association for the Advancement of Collegiate Schools of Business, the accrediting body for schools of business in the United States, there were 151,000 students attending MBA programs in this country during the 2008/2009 school year. This is in addition to the approximately two million people who have already earned an MBA.

Today's students are under enormous pressure from parents and peers to decide what it is they want to do after they graduate. As educators, our job is to remind them that they may not have the answer by then—and that that may not necessarily be a problem. When they eventually find their life's passion(s), they will already be armed with the tools to find the work they want to do.

## SURVEY RESULTS

The seven question survey targeted three groups: students who, as predicted, reported that they were not sufficiently prepared during their college years for the working world; employers who frequently complain that graduates either do not know what type of work they want to do and have little idea what skills they offer; and career counselors who lack the power to initiate systemic change and are often blamed for students' lack of career preparedness.

1.  Do you feel that college students are properly prepared for the workforce?

    80 percent answered no.

2.  What recommendations do you have that would improve students' readiness for the workforce?
    *   internships should be required (46%)
    *   mandatory career development curriculum within the general education requirements for each major (27%)
    *   liberal arts education stressing critical thinking (5%)

Other suggestions included: improved written communications, mandatory usage of career services, relevant information supplied by career services, and behavior modification.

Comments on behavior modification for Millennials included: "Many students have an entitlement mindset, and they need to be told that it is not the case anymore." "It is all about what you can offer to the company, not what they can offer you." "We are training our newer generation to expect instant gratification through technology." "I suggest more exposure to 'having to work' to earn something that is wanted or needed." "Our current way is to 'hold the hands.' Because of this, many lack the resilience to bounce back after receiving an 'F,' or after a family issue."

3. Name and describe the career preparation you received during college (counseling and/or coursework).

My subjects confirmed what I've been saying for years: higher education has systemically neglected its students' career preparation needs. Thirty percent stated that they had had none, or very little career preparation during college. A typical response: "None. And not for want of trying. I went to the counseling center at my school to figure out what I wanted to do with my degrees after I graduated and was directed to a shelf of books. I was not even sure what to do with the books. No one offered to help me and I did not know I could ask."

Another stated, "None. No career center, no coach. Might have been some books on how to put a resume together."

Since their colleges couldn't or didn't offer them the help they needed, students had to pursue career help on their own. They used a variety of resources, including courses and classes (20%). Interestingly, not all of these were career courses. The courses that helped them create their career direction were in marketing, strategy, management, communication, branding, leadership, and psychology.

The next most popular form of career preparation was a category I'll call on-the-job training, which includes volunteer opportunities, field work, work study, and internships. Seventeen percent of my subjects found these the most useful forms of career preparation. One person said, "I was working and going to school at the same time, so I was able to apply what I learned in school in my work environment. How

I applied my learning, not my degree, is what allowed me to be promoted."

Resume preparation was important to 14 percent of respondents. Unfortunately, the comment, "I only got help with my resume and cover letter. Nothing else was explained to me," was typical.

On-campus interviews and job fairs, as well as counseling with a career advisor were also considered useful.

4. To what extent do you feel you were prepared for your current or most recent position?

- very prepared (25%)
- somewhat prepared (55%)
- poorly prepared (10%)
- not prepared at all (10%)

5. What are the major areas in which you feel you were *not* prepared for your current or most recent position?

Only 9 percent said that college had prepared them for the workplace, and 65 percent said they simply were not prepared with a general, practical knowledge of how the workplace operates.

An important area for practical knowledge was *politics.* Specifically:

- "How to handle hostile work environments."
- "Maintaining my core values in the face of intense pressure."
- "Students should also be warned about the politics/issues that they will encounter as an employee and how to control them."
- "Company etiquette."
- "Working in teams."

*How to do business* was also important to respondents. For instance:

- "Business fundamentals."
- "College did not give me practical applications to what I was experiencing at work."
- "College gave me theory, tools, and things to consider, but it required my initiative to try them at work, and that was most helpful."
- "If I had received more accurate (honest) information about the employment environment, it would have been helpful."
- "The pace of learning, application, and expectations of the real world of work—*every week is finals week.*"
- "Learning how to manage client expectations, respond to their insane demands, and how to handle mistakes, screw-ups, and overall mess ups."
- "Negotiation skills."
- "Salary negotiation."
- "I was not fully prepared for the low pay and the competitiveness."
- "How much extra hard work is involved to become successful."

Learning *the difference between school and work* was helpful for some:

- "School for me was strictly academics."
- "All classes were focused on graduation requirements."
- "I was working while in high school, so everything I learned was on the job."
- "Theory is great, but that is not what is really happening in the workplace."
- Other subjects felt they lacked sufficient technology training and self-knowledge.

As a former student, Dr. Julia Fischer once told a leadership class of mine, the two things most valuable to her in life were self-awareness and the relationships she developed. Similarly, one survey subject thought it would be valuable to "learn that choosing a career direction involves considerable self-knowledge and investigation. That a career should be based on what you do well and enjoy, not just on…the subjects you excel at. I think that many twenty-one and twenty-two year olds have not had the independence and life experience to really know what they want to do."

And there were further problems: a lack of training on how to network, and no support in general. "No support from college. Preparation for my field was learned independently through trial and error and self-study."

And finally, no *mock interviews*. "I had never engaged in a mock interview—ever. Now, one of my job functions is to run mock interview workshops for college students. At first, when I began running the mock interview workshops, I felt like it was the blind leading the blind."

6. If you could do it over again, what training would you have wanted to receive during college that would have helped you adjust to and excel at your current or most recent position?

As this question was open ended and allowed the subjects to provide an unlimited number of suggestions, there were a dozen categories.

The leading category was *readiness for the workforce*.
- "Specific information on 'What can I do with a major in _____?'"
- "Every student should be required to go through a career readiness class that covers career development basics on exploration, preparation, and networking/finding the job."
- "More training in actual organizations."
- "Real world type simulation."
- "Training that puts you on the spot on a tough but safe environment."
- "More time in real-life situations practicing the skills I use so I could ask more questions of the instructors."

- "Researching companies and talking to key people within the organization."
- "Someone to really help me drill down regarding my passions and interests."
- "Skills and interests testing, followed by career potentials analysis."
- "Instruction on networking to get information and connections before unilaterally deciding a major and career."
- "Training on business practice, business management, legals, and paperwork, resume and career analysis and a list and real life examples of career options."
- "More hands-on real world experiences."
- "Dedicate one semester to job transition skills, interview techniques and job research tools."
- "Ways to network in my field of study."
- "Basic job searching skills."
- "What is expected when on the job (attitude, work ethic, hours, friends)."
- "How to perform if you want to get out of the intro position and into a higher position."
- "Most students want to be at the top and don't understand how important it is to learn from the bottom."
- "More information about career preparation."
- "Job search strategies."
- "Identification of an industry and job function they want to find employment in."
- "Coping skills."
- "How to manage oneself in the market today."
- "Ways of marketing oneself and networking (dealing realistically with one's skill set and finding jobs accordingly to build a career effectively)."
- "Personality, how you change over time."
- "Values vs. ability to do things."
- "Planning, preparation, execution."
- "Planning your career advancement stages with room for flexibility (failure is not the end, it's an opportunity to rise up)."

- "How to merge creative thinking with hard-nosed numbers/facts."
- "Motivation."
- "Interpersonal skills and passion/focus development."
- "Time spent really exploring the myriad of career choices within student's area(s) of interest."
- "Questionnaire of what they are good at and what they need help in to excel, someone to check on their progress, advice on how to get there."
- "Communication (e-mail etiquette, phone etiquette)."
- "Instruction on networking for information before jobs."
- "Helping students: find their job passion (for right now), understand the world of work in their field, evaluate the elements of a job offer, and beginning their employ in a meaningful way (it's not watching for the clock to strike 5 p.m. and tweeting all day about how boring the meeting is!)."
- "Understanding with respect to human resource management and leadership."

Some felt they would have benefited from learning *how to improve their perspective.*

- "Not training but the perspective that acknowledged learning and the growth process I would go through after college to discover my passions."
- "It would have been helpful to have an internship coordinator that sat you down and said, 'Here are some options where most students go with their degrees, pick one and explore these'...'here are some factors you may want to consider.'"
- "A greater focus on preparing for failure . . . It happens to everyone and knowing how to best deal with it would give people a greater sense of how to 'dust off, re-group, and move forward.'"
- "Self-analysis."
- "How to handle hostile work environments."

- "Realistically, if advice were given to me, I am not sure if I would have listened or paid attention. Which is the same problem with students today: those that see the relevance, pay attention and appreciate it; those that don't see an immediate relevance, don't."

Some wished they had learned more about *networking*.

- "I would receive more counseling from the career center and talk to more people who have lots of experience as well as do more networking activities."
- "Alumni, corporate, and community partnerships should be developed and maintained with the university to see the success of a graduate to fruition in their area of study/profession."
- "Meeting with executives and interviewers and listening to exactly what they look for in hiring someone."
- "Job search and networking training, role-playing exercises, etc."
- "I know a number of instances where undergraduates successfully secure—and excel—in internships that result in job offers/employment upon graduation. But for many, not only is there a lack of focus and direction, but an inability to effectively use job-search resources."
- "Phone screening and interview training, more role-playing exercises, and training in follow-up correspondence."
- "Be able to present yourself, network, and learn about what social groups to join."
- "Help these students connect to specific individuals in their desired fields and track their progress with these executives/experts, not merely giving them websites to use."
- "University corporate partnerships with hiring managers (direct contact from university to that manager)."
- "More research of what companies are doing in that field, more engagement with professional associations."

- "I would regularly practice professional networking that would include mock interviewing, field trips to chosen professions, presentations from chosen professions, and internship requirements."

Some respondents advocated for more *internships and job shadowing*:

- "Internship, job shadowing for exploration, more exposure to the many ways I could use my knowledge/degree."
- "Definitely hands-on training in a few areas so that I can get a good feel for at least three areas I was interested in getting into."
- "Provide resources to identify internships and stipends so all students could afford summer internships."
- "Actually having students volunteer/intern for perhaps for ten weeks of a twelve-week semester."
- "Education in and outside the classroom to build competencies. This would necessarily include practical application (which gives exposure)."
- "I went to a university that required all of us to serve in the community every year thus allowing us to build/hone skills, redirect, and create a network and references for future work."
- "Mandatory internships for all students."
- "In the field practicum."
- "Observation of actual workplaces."
- "What working in an office/your potential place of work is really like."
- "Visits/shadow programs/internships—short and long— to get a real feel of different industries/environments."
- "Required internships, required project for a company, field trips."
- "Internship/volunteer work."
- "Learning at professional work setting."
- "Reality check—what working in an office/your potential place of work is really like."

- "Internship involvement to provide actual experience in the chosen field of interest."

Some recommended more *mentoring*.

- "More hands-on activities in the classroom such as interaction with business professionals and learning from their experiences at their workplaces."
- "We did not have that many guest speakers during my school years."
- "Mentorship at an earlier stage."
- "Assign mentors in two to three different industries/ functions, arrange 'ride days' with mentors to show expectations."
- "Mentorship/apprenticeship."
- "Work assignments and interaction with career mentors who have experience in the positions the student aspires to hold."
- "Guest speakers from all types of businesses."

Many wished they'd had more training in *financial management*, including salary negotiation.

- "Better and earlier understanding of financial management issues."
- "Accounting skills and how to deal with financial and budgetary aspects of a career."
- "Understanding of global economics."
- "Impact of financial management on decision making."

Others wished they'd had more *interview preparation* and *resume workshops* that included development of cover letters, thank-you letters, LinkedIn profiles, and e-mail correspondence skills.

Some wished there had been more *courses*, including those in communications, business fundamentals, public speaking skills, writing, interviewing, networking, interpersonal communication, marketing, career management, global business, and presentation skills.

Some wished there'd been more *career testing.*

- "The most important thing I could have received was a skills and interest assessment so I could pursue something that would be fulfilling and not have to wait thirty years to get there."
- "Assessment (fascination, skills and values) and exploration to choose a likely career direction and course of study."
- "Take a test and interview the student to determine what his interests are and what he would like to be doing as a career."
- "Assessment of students' readiness to make a career decision at this time: undergrads are young."

7. If you were designing a career development program for an undergraduate student, what would be its three major elements?

In order of popularity, suggestions were:

1. Field experience (internships, field training, community service)
2. Personal development/coping skills
3. Networking and job search techniques
4. Developing written marketing materials (resumes, cover letters, thank-you letters, LinkedIn profiles)
5. Counseling
6. Mentoring
7. Coursework
8. Financial literacy and negotiating skills
9. Selling/branding
10. Corporate culture and politics
11. Assessment testing
12. Informational interviews

## SUMMARY OF THE SURVEY

Eighty percent of the survey subjects said that students were not properly prepared for the workforce. Any other program in higher education which failed eight out of ten students would require a major revision in its structure and delivery methods, so revising the way colleges and universities administer career education is certainly an idea whose time has come.

When asked what they recommended to improve students' readiness, 46 percent of subjects named internships, and 27 percent said mandatory courses. The program I recommend is mandatory, and internships are a required part of the curriculum, beginning during a student's sophomore year.

As to what career preparation the subjects received during their undergraduate years, 30 percent received none at all, and only 12 percent received counseling. The career course program will address these issues.

How prepared for the working world did our subjects report they felt by the time they graduated college? Twenty percent said that they were either "poorly prepared," or "not prepared at all."

When asked to name the specific areas in which they felt unprepared, 75 percent said "general knowledge." Given it begins during a student's freshman year, my career course program will continually provide an overview of the working world and teach the student to use his or her skill set and experience to find their place in it.

Asked if they had it to do over again, subjects said their career training in college would consist of, in order of preference: readiness, improved perspective, networking, internships/job shadowing, mentoring, money management, interview preparation, resume workshops, and courses. All of these have been embedded into the program curriculum that follows. This relates to the final question in the survey, in which the subjects were asked to name three elements they would include in redesigning a career development program.

The five most often cited elements were: field experience, personal development, networking, written materials, and counseling.

All of these are included in the design of the career development course program.

The great dichotomy in the jobseeking process in the twenty-first century is that one needs a flawless resume, an excellent cover letter, and a degree—yet none of those, nor all of them together, even ensures an interview. Contrary to its importance in the last century, the resume is simply a marketing document, a script for one's sales pitch. Cover letters are not necessarily read, and a degree has less value than it once did. Finding a job has become the same process as getting a date; one needs to develop a sense of relatedness, mutual interest, trust, and opportunity before one can get a job—or a date. This is why networking skills are the foundation of the entire process.

The career course program emphasizes social skills, as students, particularly those in the Millennial generation, have a reputation for being ineffective at communicating both orally and in writing.

Additional training includes encouraging students to learn the language of the industry in which they choose to work. It is critical that they constantly read and learn about developments in that industry. Given employers hire people with whom they are comfortable and can trust, it is essential that students are perceived as being part of that culture.

Lastly, students are advised to prepare themselves for incremental career growth. With family pressure to decide on a career and quickly repay school loans, it is critical that as educators, we direct our students to find how they can be of service to employers in *some* capacity, trusting that with hard work, time, and the appropriate alliances, they can eventually realize their career dreams.

# CHAPTER TEN

# THE CAREER DEVELOPMENT COURSE PROGRAM

Learning in the twenty-first century is no longer simply about the passive absorption of information. Students need to be stimulated by the environment and connect with what is being presented in order for learning to take place. Learning is more than conveying information to others; it's about gaining *knowledge,* about practical and relevant material that the student can use in his or her life.

Experiential learning, the foundation of everything I teach, is defined as "the process whereby knowledge is created through transformation of experience" (Kolb). One of my goals in designing the career development course program is to create an environment in which students can be active learners.

The context for my program is: corporate loyalty and job security are becoming extinct. In the twenty-first century workplace, we all are freelancers and thus our own brand. In my program, students learn how to determine, articulate, and then market that brand in order to continue to find work throughout their entire career. In other words, the program empowers students to develop the resources needed for the lifelong practice of self-promotion.

In order to properly train students for this radically altered workplace, there must be a radically new approach to training them: coursework needs to be mandatory, begin during freshman year and continuing through the end of senior year, and be delivered in conjunction with required one-on-one counseling.

The career course program will have students work to develop particular competencies, and part of every class will be spent on rehearsing these skills. It's my firm belief that learning that lasts and changes behavior, particularly when it involves communication skills, is best accomplished through practice. Hence, though there are hundreds of books available that tell you "how to," rehearsing the skills will create "muscle memory." Students primarily learn (indeed, anyone learns) by doing - over and over and over again.

By the time students complete the program, they will:

1. Define their brand and its uniqueness in the marketplace.
2. Be adept at articulating their message to the people who can hire or refer them for work.
3. Have developed a granular database.
4. Have a resume and bio that reflects what they offer and serves as a powerful marketing tool.
5. Appreciate the employer's perspective and use that to better direct their sales efforts.
6. Have less anxiety about both the interview process and negotiating.
7. Be aware of the other life skills they will need to navigate the world (knowledge of sexual harassment guidelines, financial planning, business cards, a web site, social networking, et cetera).
8. Have made a permanent practice of reading about current and future trends in their industry.

Based on the results of my study, the program begins with the incoming class of first-year students. Using a semester system with three semesters per school year, in the four years a student attends college, they will have completed twelve semesters of coursework, so there are twelve courses in the career development program. The number and frequency of classes can be adjusted to the needs of any higher learning institution. For example, some schools are on a term system, whereas others have four semesters per school year; the program design is flexible enough to expand or contract based on the school's schedules.

It is also appropriate for integration into graduate programs, although beginning the training with younger students will ultimately have a greater impact. There are those who believe that career training should begin as early as middle school. While it's probably a good idea to introduce the concept of career planning when students are twelve or thirteen years old, a formal program will be more effective if it's begun somewhat later in a student's life.

Students will take the courses according to the following schedule.

**Freshman year, first semester: "101 Introduction to the Twenty-first Century Workplace: You Are a Freelancer"** The twentieth century version of employment (a job at one company for decades, retirement with a pension) is now the exception. You are on your own, and you have your own brand. You will learn to design and manage your career; you will examine what it is you are selling, who your market is, how you reach potential employers, and what you tell them when you meet them.

**Freshman year, second semester: "102 Determining Your Monetizeable Passion"** Choosing a career direction involves considerable self-knowledge and investigation. A career should be based on what you do well and enjoy. You will examine what it is you want to do by answering the questions, what service or services am I offering? And is there a market for it? In-class exercises will help you determine your professional niche. You will drill down to find your passion(s) during required individual meetings with your career counselor, which will be run in conjunction with the course.

Following are exercises designed to enable students to locate what they really love to do that can be offered as a paid service to others (Pope & Minor, 2000)

*Career Fantasies*

Think back on your very first dream careers, then continue to think from this point onward through your personal history, recapturing fantasy pictures you have had of yourself in various careers. Keep a list...beginning with your earliest career fantasy, of the names of the occupations you've fantasized about...

Now go through your list, looking for possible interest patterns that reoccur (i.e., one-to-one interactions with others, producing a product, persuading and motivating others, and being physically active).

Also, make notes for yourself about desirable features of the types of work you are considering and the environments that your fantasy career choices typically occur in (i.e., working on my own without interruptions, having people look to me as "the expert" for advice, and operating in a busy, varied work environment).

*Values Auction*

This exercise is designed to help make the student conscious of his or her values and priorities. They are symbolically given a large sum of money and asked to allocate their funds to "bid" on the items they want most. These items (with their symbolic meanings in parentheses) include:

- to be elected to a position of leadership (professional recognition)
- the ability to rid the world of unfairness and inequality (social justice)
- a complete library of the great books of the world with personal access to all the people who wrote them (wisdom)
- the perfect partnership/relationship (intimate relationship)
- to reach a state of perfect fitness and to live to be one hundred years old (health and long life)

- to be the artistic genius of my time in music, literature, or art (creativity)
- the ability to set my own working conditions, write my own "perfect job" description, and then fill it (freedom and personal autonomy)
- unlimited travel with passes to all activities in every part of the world (adventure and risk-taking)
- perfect insight into the meaning of life and harmony with all life (inner peace and spiritual harmony)
- to achieve the highest level in my chosen career field (sense of accomplishment)
- the ability to remove all threats to world peace (world peace)
- a close circle of loyal friends throughout life (friendship)
- a society where people do things the right way (consistency and order)
- perfect loving and harmonious family relations (family affection, support, and security)
- to be the world's wealthiest person (financial security and economic independence)
- a free lifetime pass to the ultimate luxury resort where all my needs are anticipated and met (leisure and comfort)
- to always speak and hear the truth (honesty)
- the opportunity to better the lives of others (service to others)
- to know I can do and be whatever I want (self-confidence)
- to achieve my own goals as a result of hard work (self discipline).

*The Dream Vacation Activity*

This is a visualization activity...you have won a dream vacation. You can go anywhere and do anything...Picture a place in your mind right now, with you there. Where is this place? Is it a place you have not been to, or a place you have visited before? What attracts you to this place?

You can bring one person with you, if you wish. Would you go alone or have a travel companion? If you would go with some-one, picture that person with you at your destination, enjoying the sites and relaxation just as you do. Why did you choose this person?

Pay close attention to the destinations as they relate to future careers, the travel companions as they relate to future types of co-workers, and transportation and accommodations as they relate to future work settings.

Presumably after doing one of more of these exercises, the applicant will have a good idea of his or her monetizeable passion, or at least an idea of what kind of work they could do. Now he or she is ready to create their brand.

**Freshman year, third semester: "103 You, the Brand: What Are Your Sell Points?"** You will create, refine, and practice your sound bite in front of the class. This is your primary marketing tool and you will become comfortable saying it to everyone you meet, as you never know who may be in a position to offer you work or a referral. Your sound bite will tell the listener what you offer and what you are looking for in the short term.

**Sophomore year, first semester: "201 The Employer's Perspective"** Once you better understand your audience, you can gear your pitch to make it more effective. In this course, you will begin to focus on the employer's needs and learn compassion for their perspective in the hiring process. We will also create a schedule for your three required internships during your next three years of college, all of which must relate directly to your field of interest.

**Sophomore year, second semester: "202 Developing Your Story"** The extension of your sound bite are your stories: a series of interesting and engaging stories about your life and passions. Imagine your life is a movie with you as the star. Your story is the narrative of how you got to where you are in your career and your goals for the future. You will develop these stories and enrich them with details, and then continually practice telling them to your peers in the classroom until you have become comfortable with the process of selling yourself.

**Sophomore year, third semester: "203 Networking and Creating a Granular Database"** Students are continually encouraged to network, but seldom are you properly trained on exactly what that is or how to go about it. Networking is making friends for the purpose of forwarding your career, and the course will train you in this lifelong practice. We will begin with a portable, electronic, granular database, the foundation for all networking. You will create an initial database of leads and then develop those leads. We will discuss the value of social networks, including LinkedIn, Facebook, and Twitter, and of joining and volunteering for professional associations in your field. You will be assigned mandatory meetings with your career counselor throughout the remainder of your college years, which you will schedule during this course. We will discuss mentoring and job shadowing, and you will be assigned Industry Leader Interview papers as a way to begin those processes. You will start at the top and aim high: who are the stars of your industry that you've dreamed of meeting? You will target them for face-to-face meetings to learn how they became successful and what you need to do to become successful yourself.

# HOW I GOT MY START IN THE DIGITAL MEDIA INDUSTRY

I was working in video post production sales in the early 1990s and began reading about interactive multimedia, and saw it as the next big thing (this was prior to the Internet). I didn't even own a computer, but that didn't stop me. I began calling people I knew (this was also prior to e-mail) and asking if they knew anyone in the field. Most of them had no idea what interactive multimedia even was, but I kept calling until I found one colleague who did. She said that the leading association in the field was called the International Interactive Communications Society (IICS), that it numbered five thousand members worldwide, most of whom were educators who worked with laser discs, and that they had a chapter in Los Angeles, where I was—and am—based. She gave me a phone number. I called and learned that the Los Angeles chapter was holding a meeting in a couple of weeks at the home of one of its members.

There were ten people at the meeting. The chapter was going through a rough patch; attendance was down and they were thinking of closing. They needed new chapter officers and when the vice presidential slot was mentioned, I volunteered. I was told that one of my duties would be producing the chapter's monthly meetings, which was considered an onerous task.

I, on the other hand, was elated. I'd been sending my resume and calling the multimedia departments of the major movie studios in order to find a job. Given I had zero experience, I'd been completely ignored. Suddenly, I was transformed from a wannabe in the field into "Chaz Austin, Vice President, Los Angeles chapter, International Interactive Communications Society." I went back to all the studios. They now took my calls and I was able to offer them something: the opportunity to showcase their newest product or service to our chapter membership of one hundred working professionals. Everyone said yes to my invitation.

At every meeting, I stood at the door and welcomed our guests from the studios as a colleague, not as a jobseeker. That's how I built my database and a lucrative consulting practice in interactive marketing and business development that sustained itself for eight years, until I began teaching.

Joining associations in your field of choice is a start, but volunteering is better. Volunteering allows you to spend time working with people in your field (in my case, producing meetings) and giving them the opportunity to see you in action. This will lead to paid work. Think of it from the employer's perspective: they have a job opening. They have a choice of interviewing strangers, or hiring someone they know and have worked with. What would you do in their position?

**Junior year, first semester: "301 The Resume: Your Primary Marketing Document."** You will create a resume and a bio that reflect who you are in the workplace. Your work will be edited by your classmates and your professor.

**Junior year, second semester: "302 Budgeting"** Everyone is a freelancer with his or her own business and/or brand. Financial liquidity is critical to sustaining that brand. A working budget is essential during the downtimes between jobs. In this course, you will learn to distinguish needs from wants, create a budget listing your expenses and income, and explore ways to increase revenue and cut expenses.

**Junior year, third semester: "303 Interviewing"** You will rehearse how to interview in front of your classmates. You will be given questions you can expect to be asked in formal interviews and begin to formulate your answers. The mock interviews, conducted by the professor, other students, and industry professionals, are one of the most valuable parts of your career development program. Industry guests will inform you what they look for when hiring, and there will be opportunities to develop mentoring relationships and job shadowing opportunities.

**Senior year, first semester: "401 Interviewing the Employer"** In an interview, part of your job is to learn if the potential employer is a good fit for *you*. The better your brand self-awareness, the more confidence you will exude and the easier it will be for you to question the employer's appropriateness to your needs.

**Senior year, second semester: "402 Cover and Thank-You Letters"** In this course, you will dissect job descriptions and practice writing cover letters that are short and to the point using the three-paragraph approach: the connection, the match, and the next step.

**Senior year, third semester: "403 Negotiating"** What do you ask for when you're offered a job or want to ask for a raise? This course explores negotiating from a position of strength, not desperation, and the benefits to consider beyond a salary. We will learn, explore, and practice your own negotiating skills.

## PROGRAM IMPLEMENTATION

In higher education, career development is perceived as *vocational*, as opposed to traditional coursework, which is seen as *academic*. In the traditional, academic approach, higher education is a way for the student to expand their perspective on the world and develop and improve their ability to think critically. College is not seen as a place to develop practical skills or prepare someone for the workforce. On the contrary, it's a safe place removed from mundane, everyday concerns like earning a living and paying the bills.

In the newer, vocational approach to a college education, college serves as a trade school, a place where you are prepared to enter the workforce and where you are taught practical skills with which you can earn money in your chosen field. Thus, philosophy, history, and the classics are avoided because they will not get you a job; they are considered largely a waste of time.

My program synthesizes these two approaches.

There is some resistance among academics about the suitability of including career courses in a student's college experience. Because meeting and working with career counselors is not required, and only a limited number of courses are being offered at this time to train students in how to self-market, the general perception is that career counseling is simply an extra service, like the school nurse or soft drinks available at the campus bookstore. They make the college experience more pleasant, but are not an essential part of a student's education.

Some members of a college administration will consider an entire career course program to be a radical departure from tradition, and resist its implementation. Just as students in the program are trained to approach their career growth incrementally, given this expected resistance, career coursework can be rolled out over time, if necessary. This will serve to mitigate the dislocation that staff or faculty may feel. The courses in the new program will replace existing courses, and educators are reluctant to give up their classes, particularly if they feel that what is supplanting them is not appropriate for the classroom. A slow rollout will also make it easier to fine-tune the program.

The efficacy of career development coursework must be demonstrated to deans, department chairs, and faculty, so I suggest these courses be rolled out on a test basis. The process would begin with a few sessions included in an existing course; for example, a marketing course could contain sessions on self-marketing.

Surveys of participating students would be conducted at the end of the course to determine the effectiveness of the career sessions. The career courses I have taught have met with unanimous approval from students, and the dozens of endorsements I've received illustrate the effectiveness and applicability of this work:

Elizabeth Ishii

I just got a job at Lapis and I'm going to be the Assistant Designer. I am so excited, especially getting the job within a week of graduating from your course. My new boss told me that my resume was unlike all the others he received.

Kenny Cogo

Your class really taught me a lot. The constant mock interviews are genius. Your concept of social networking is what I have always thought is the best way to find work because it's not just about what you know, it's who you know. I got this interview through one of my contacts that I made through your class, so your methods work, and work well.

Joseph Kim

I wasn't sure what to expect when I first found out I had Career Development as one of my classes. However I have to admit it was one of my favorite classes, and the most useful. Thank you for your insight.

Tom Smith

The Post Production Marketplace & Job Essentials that you taught was probably the most useful and important class that I attended. The information, ideas, and techniques presented in the workshop have really helped point me in the right direction.

I no longer simply 'look for a job' but rather attempt to engage in the marketing, branding, and promotion of the services that I can provide. I particularly appreciated your up-beat, can-do, no-nonsense attitude, which I found to be inspiring and motivating especially during those moments of uncertainty and self doubt that inevitably arise at the start of any considerable endeavor.

Erik Bleitz
Professor Austin is concise, honest, and upfront. I spoke to him in the morning and landed a job that evening by doing exactly what he recommended.

Gabriela Caro
You gave me a sense of empowerment...and how to focus my knowledge and experience where it will best be utilized in making me happy. I gained a lot of confidence in myself.

Danielle Keller
I am going to start interning for Fashion Biz Inc. in two weeks. I also have already written an article for their newsletter. I just wanted to say thank you for all your help. I am so excited to really start my career.

Ross Van Voast
I wanted to let you know the career development class was awesome and a great inspiration for me. I realized building your brand is most of the battle.

Michael Tanenbaum
Professor Austin understands the importance and power of networking and personal selling, skills which cannot be underestimated in today's professional marketplace.

Angela Copeland
Professor Austin is a life-changing career coach. He identified potential opportunities for me that lined up perfectly with my goals and encouraged me to lay my foundation for a success-

ful future. He goes above and beyond any typical career coach to help his clients put life-changing strategies into motion.

Lilian P. Baghdasarian
You make me feel much better every time I walk out of your office with an inspiring hope of a brighter future in my career.

Mychelle Lozano
This was a great class...enriching and very informative because Prof. Austin shared so much of his knowledge. It was exceptionally educational and fascinating...it introduced me to the importance of planning, social and ethical responsibilities, and the changes that are shaping today's workplace. Prof. Austin gave me broad-based, valuable insights and a practical introduction to the key ideas that I will be able to use for years to come.

Leandro Ramos
I learned who I really am and who I will be.

Once the career sessions have proven effective, they can be expanded to stand-alone courses. After those are delivered, further surveys should be conducted. After analyzing the predicted positive results, the administration and faculty will find that these courses are popular with students, increase retention to graduation, reflect positively on the institution, and are cost-effective because they train students how to find work, and employed graduates tend to be more generous in gift-giving to their alma mater. At that point, a full career course program can be established.

Dr. David Rosen, the Senior Vice President and chief academic officer at Woodbury University, with whom I worked to design and implement the program, described the early stages of its development: "During the fall board retreat, I saw a print-out of a presentation that Charles had prepared on a new plan for career development. I found Charles' plan refreshingly different and likely to be effective. Immediately after the retreat, I contacted Charles to get a copy of the presentation. We sat for nearly an hour reviewing his work. I was impressed with his ideas.

From that moment, Charles and I joined forces to look for ways to implement his new model for career development. When the opportunity for a Walmart grant to support a career development curriculum arose, I asked Charles to be on the team to prepare the grant. His research and ideas were helpful in creating a successful proposal."

# CONCLUSION

It is time to elevate career development to parity with other academic disciplines. The traditional model for delivering career services is outmoded, inefficient, and wasteful. Career counselors cannot accomplish much in an hour-long meeting with a student, yet given working with a career counselor is not mandatory, that is often as much time as a counselor will have with that student. If career courses are a mandatory part of the curriculum, regular visits with the counselor can also be made mandatory, and these one-on-one sessions can have a lasting impact.

The training I am advocating will teach students to develop practices they can use to advance their careers for as long as they work. Institutions of higher learning will benefit in numerous ways, as well. Studies have shown that career development courses are a cost-effective intervention. When academic credit is involved, the institution almost always stands to benefit, because retention rates increase.

A college student who is taught over time how to sell their brand will be more likely to have work when they graduate. An employed graduate is a happy alumnus. A happy alumnus repays his or her alma mater in donations, thus reducing the workload of the college's advancement/development department. Knowing that the alma mater prepares its students for the workplace, the same alum will be more likely to offer jobs, internships, and mentoring, thus saving time for the college's career development department. All this will forge stronger ties between the school and its alumni, one of the primary goals of any institution of higher learning. Conversely, and unfortunately, an alum who isn't working will often blame the school for his or her failure to find employment.

By training students how to monetize their education, a growing concern to both students and their families, a value-add is provided for the college or university that will help differentiate their brand from other institutions of higher learning.

My survey (and other studies reporting the success of courses and similar, though more limited, programs) suggests an idea whose time has come. I predict that the effectiveness of this program will result in career development coursework being embedded into the general college curriculum in every institution of higher learning in the United States in the next decade.

Integrating career development coursework in this manner will be a boon to students, the universities at which they study, and the organizations for which they will eventually work. A student population that is better prepared for work can make a more positive impact on the world.

Made in the USA
San Bernardino, CA
21 December 2012